A
COMMONSENSE
GUIDE TO
Mutual
FUNDS

A
COMMONSENSE
GUIDE TO

Mutual FUNDS

MARY ROWLAND

Bloomberg Press

◆

PRINCETON

Bloomberg Press books are available for bulk purchases at special discounts for educational, business, or sales promotional use. Special editions or book excerpts can also be created to specifications. For information please write: Special Markets Department, Bloomberg Press, 100 Business Park Drive, P.O. Box 888, Princeton, NJ 08542-0888, U.S.A.

Library of Congress Catalog Card Number 96-83201

ISBN 1-57660-000-9

Bloomberg Press books are printed on acid-free paper.

This publication is designed to provide accurate and authoritative information. It is sold with the understanding that the publisher is not engaged in rendering legal, accounting, investment planning, or other professional services. If legal advice or other expert assistance is required, the services of a competent professional person should be sought.

First edition published 1996

1 3 5 7 9 10 8 6 4 2

Book Design by Don Morris Design

To

Krista

and

Thomas

— **M.R.**

INTRODUCTION 1

PART 1
The Dos and Don'ts
Here are 60 points of wisdom that you can use immediately to make your money work smarter. **8**

PART 2
Building Blocks
The history of mutual funds, and what you need to know to buy and sell. **130**

PART 3
Risk and Asset Allocation
How aggressive should you be? And once you decide, how do you spread your money around? **152**

PART 4
Commonsense Strategies
Discipline is the key to these simple plans used by successful strategic investors. **188**

PART 5
Resources
In print, on-line, and by phone: how to find information to help you make smart choices. **210**

INDEX 220

INTRODUCTION

ANOTHER BOOK on mutual funds? Funds promised to simplify investing for Americans, yet they grow ever more complex. Nearly 2,000 new funds were introduced in 1995. Today there are almost 8,000 funds. Certainly there's no shortage of information available about mutual funds. Yet surveys continue to show that even though 40 million Americans own them, most investors don't understand what they own.

Nearly everyone needs to know the basics about mutual funds. You might need to know how to choose investments

for a 401(k) plan, how to invest money
from an insurance or divorce settlement,
or how to get started as an investor. But
you probably don't want to plow through
a mutual fund textbook. And you don't
need to. You need a concise guide to
mutual fund investing.

I wrote a mutual fund book a half
dozen years ago. As a result of that book, a
mutual fund column I write for *Bloomberg
Personal*, and a personal finance column
that I wrote for *The New York Times* every
Sunday for five years, I have received thousands of letters from readers asking for

investing advice. What I have gleaned from these letters is that people don't want generic information. They want more advice; they want to know which funds to buy and which funds to avoid.

That's why Part 1 provides DOs and DON'Ts. One could quibble that the device is too simplistic. Or too opinionated. But the letters I get hammer home the point that investors want those things.

If you have some experience in mutual funds, dip right into the DOs and DON'Ts. Start anywhere. Read anything that catches your eye. For example:

DON'T jump in just before a fund closes to new investors.

DO manage your own cash.

DON'T buy bond funds.

DO take a skeptical attitude toward mutual fund ratings.

DON'T ignore new funds.

If you are a beginner and need to start with the basics, read Part 2: Building Blocks and Part 3: Risk and Asset Allocation before you start the DOs and DON'Ts. Part 4: Commonsense Strategies describes some investment strategies. And Part 5: Resources provides additional resources for mutual fund investors.

The result is a guide that takes a strong, authoritative view. It is based on my 22 years of reporting and writing about business and personal finance, as well as the fresh research I did on mutual funds for this book. I learned a good deal while researching and writing it, including some things that helped me become a better investor.

I hope you will learn something about yourself and what kind of investor you are, as well as how to set goals and develop strategies for investing in mutual

funds. Mutual funds are the best investment vehicle available today. What you
get out of them can mean the difference
between a comfortable lifestyle and just
scraping by.

◆ A note about the design of this book:
In the text of the **DOs AND DON'Ts** section,
you will find financial terms set in a
BLACK BAR ; these correspond to defi-
nitions found at the bottom of that page.
An arrow in the margin directs you to
another page in the book on which you
will find a longer discussion of that term.

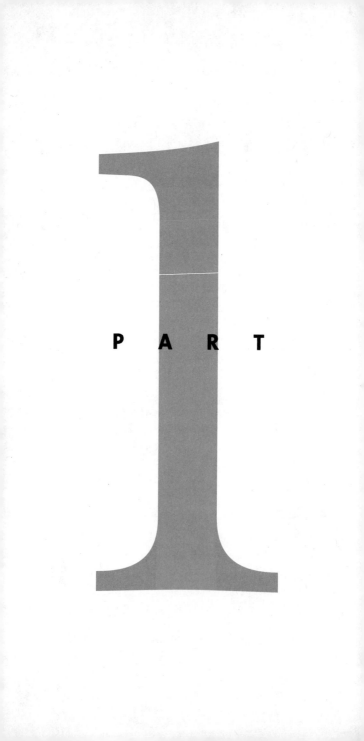

PART

1

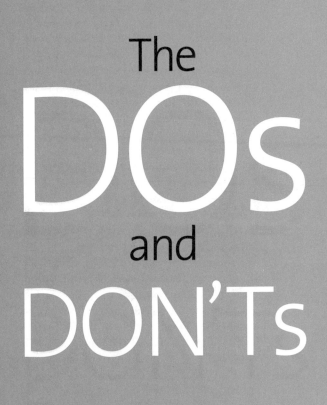

The
DOs
and
DON'Ts

DO invest chiefly in the stock market.

Stocks provide the best performance over time. Period. Everyone has heard the statistics by now. So why doesn't everyone plow all his money into stocks? Because of the stock market's volatility in the short term. Stocks do not beat bonds and money market funds every year. Investors who need some money over the short term for retirement income, college tuition, or a down payment on a house should not have all their money in stocks. But long-term investors should put the bulk of their assets in a variety of stock funds, including international funds, and some more-conservative income funds.

Before you put your money in stocks, prepare for a bumpy ride, including some years when you would have been better off with your money under the mattress. For example, in 1994, money market investments beat both stocks and bonds. Sometimes the stock market has a bad run for several years in a row. Or it might be up 25 percent one year and down 5 percent the next. That's what investors call **VOLATILITY**, which means moving quickly and unpredictably.

Still, the course of the market is ever upward. Consider the movement of the **DOW JONES AVERAGE** of 30 industrials, which is often used as a measure of the market.

THE DOW JONES INDUSTRIAL AVERAGE *Reflects the movement of 30 large-company stocks. Although it is the most widely quoted index, these stocks do not always move in sync with the broader market or the market for small-company stocks.*

Some professionals argue that you would do best to be out of stocks when they dive and in the stock market when they're soaring. That may be true, but no one has consistently predicted those swings. Those investors who try to guess when stocks will do well and when they will do poorly lose out. When you consider the path of the Dow, you can see there are periods when it languishes. It took 13 years—from 1972 to 1985—for it to climb just 500 points, from 1,000 to 1,500. But there are times when it soars, often unexpectedly, as in late 1990 and early 1991, when it rebounded following fears about war in the Middle East.

Consider this: The Dow finished 1993—a respectable year when the **STANDARD & POOR'S 500** gained 10 percent—at just over 3,700. The following year was pretty unremarkable, with the S&P returning just 1.31 percent and the Dow making little progress. Many discouraged investors contemplated getting out of stocks by the end of 1994. In 1995, the market exploded, gaining 37.5 percent. In early 1996, it passed three 100-point marks in only six sessions to reach 5,600.

Investing in stocks—and in stock mutual funds—does require research. But it is not akin to gambling, as some fearful investors claim. Among the thousands of mutual funds available, there are dozens of fine performers with strong, consistent records of 10 years or more. They make a good starting point.

Finally, here are the numbers: From 1960 to 1995, the compound annual return on stocks was 10.7 percent; on bonds, 7.4 percent; on Treasury bills, 6.0 percent (stocks measured by the S&P 500 index, bonds by long-term governments, and T-bills of 30-day maturity).

DON'T buy bond funds.

Sure it's a broad-brush generalization. Obviously there are some circumstances in which a bond fund will do. But most investors buying bond funds could do better elsewhere. Even those looking for income can find alternatives.

Bonds hold less return potential than stocks—a good two percentage points less on average, according to Sanford C. Bernstein & Co., a Wall Street research house. But when you put a bond in a bond fund, you run into some additional problems.

Bond funds carry high **EXPENSES**. In 1994, the average municipal bond fund carried expenses of .85 percent; the average corporate bond fund .92 percent; the average government bond fund .99 percent; and the average international bond fund 1.46 percent, according to **MORNINGSTAR MUTUAL FUNDS**, the Chicago mutual funds rating company.

A study by New York bond dealers Gabriele, Hueglin & Cashman comparing yields (the coupon rate of interest divided by the purchase price) on individual bonds, unit investment trusts, and bond mutual funds found that bond funds consistently underperformed the other two, sometimes by more than 2 percent a year, as they did in 1980 and 1981. The funds' fees depressed their yields year after year, making them "less attractive the longer they are held," according to the study.

MORNINGSTAR *The best source of consumer information on mutual funds, including performance data, analysis, and a rating system ranging from zero to five stars. For information on publications available, see Part 5: Resources.*

Bond funds are inconsistent performers, making it impossible to select one winner from a bad batch, according to a study by Lewis J. Altfest, a financial planner and professor at Pace University in New York City. "There are no Peter Lynches in the bond market," Altfest says. "There are no bond funds that consistently outperform the average." A study by Altfest found that other mutual funds showed some consistency in performance, but bond funds did not. "One bond fund manager was just as good as another. And no one could outperform the indexes," Altfest says.

Few funds offer unique strategies. "The thing that gives a mutual fund its franchise— the quality of management—plays a smaller role in bond funds," says Morningstar president Don Phillips. "The best bond fund manager might turn in 11 percent and the worst 9 percent." In contrast, stock fund performance might range from +95 percent to −40 percent.

Bond funds don't allow you to target your own goals or employ your own strategies. If you buy a bond fund because you think bonds are good value now compared with stocks, or because you think interest rates will fall and **BOND PRICES** will rise, the bond manager can defeat you by moving into shorter-term bonds. 199

Investors looking for income might try some funds with a mix of high-dividend stocks, preferred stocks, utilities, and, sometimes, **REITS**, 98 which invest in real estate. Candidates: Berwyn Income, Lindner Dividend, USAA Income Stock, Vanguard/Wellesley Income, Boston Co. Managed Income. Finally, two acceptable bond funds: Spectrum Income, from T. Rowe Price, or a short-maturity (under five years) fund like Vanguard Short-Term Bond.

DO build your portfolio with at least three "core" mutual funds.

The core should represent at least 50 percent of your holdings. Once you've established it, you can build around it. But don't get carried away—just a few will do. Consider three areas: stocks with a large **MARKET CAPITALIZATION**, small-company stocks, and international stocks.

Large-cap U.S. funds should represent 25 to 50 percent of a long-term portfolio. If you have already started a portfolio with a balanced fund like Vanguard/Wellington, it can serve as a large-cap core holding. If not, an obvious choice is the Vanguard Index 500. Other possibilities: Dodge & Cox Stock, Harbor Capital Appreciation, or Vanguard/Windsor II.

Small-cap funds should represent 12 to 25 percent of a long-term portfolio. Picking a good fund in this category is one of the toughest exercises for an investor because few funds are solid long-term performers. When a fund establishes a great track record, assets explode and the manager often can't find enough good small companies to buy.

That leaves you with two possible solutions. The first is to pick an index fund like Vanguard Extended Market Index, which invests in the Wilshire 4500, representing all the stocks that are traded on exchanges minus the **STANDARD & POOR'S 500**, or the Vanguard

---

MARKET CAPITALIZATION *The total value the market puts on a company. It is calculated by multiplying the price of a stock by the total number of shares. Big-cap stocks have market values of more than $10 billion; small-caps generally have values less than $500 million; medium-caps are in between.*

Index Small-Cap Stock fund, which follows the Russell 2000. Index funds do not attempt to select the best of the small companies. So they will not do as well as a good small-cap manager, but they will beat a bad small-cap manager. If you are not willing to work on your investments, consider an index fund.

Another choice is to get in on the ground floor with a good small-cap fund. For example, Garrett Van Wagoner, a manager with a red-hot three-year record at Govett Smaller Companies fund, left at year-end 1995 to set up his own group of funds. Newsletters like *The No-Load Fund Investor* or *Morningstar Investor* follow these developments.

International-stock funds should represent 12 to 25 percent of a long-term portfolio. Look for a pure international play that includes investment in Japan. You should understand the distinction between these funds and global funds, which invest all over the world, including the U.S. Because you are picking your own U.S. funds, you want an international fund that excludes the U.S.

There are many international funds with good, solid long-term records, including T. Rowe Price International Stock, Scudder International, Templeton Foreign, Vanguard International Growth, and Warburg Pincus International Equity. SoGen International is classified as an **ASSET ALLOCATION FUND**, but it is a solid core portfolio holding.

32

STANDARD & POOR'S 500 *An index of 500 widely held stocks that is often used as a proxy for the overall market. It includes 400 industrial companies, 40 financial companies, 40 public utilities, and 20 transportation companies.*

DON'T buy alphabet soup funds (B shares, C shares, M shares, Y shares).

The simpler, the better is the rule. If you must buy a load fund, or one that charges a commission, get one with a front-end load and no 12b-1 fee. You're better off with a straightforward, up-front haircut on your investment than little nibbles over the years.

When you buy a fund from a broker, you pay a sales charge or commission, supposedly for the advice he offers. These commissions have been around as long as mutual funds. But in 1980, the Securities and Exchange Commission (SEC) wrote Rule 12b-1, authorizing fund companies to add a new annual charge for marketing and distribution, which might include advertising costs or an annual payout to the broker who sold you the fund. This fee, like the fund's other **EXPENSES**, is deducted each and every year from the fund's assets.

In the mid-1980s, as investors began to resist paying commissions to buy funds, two big fund groups devised a way to hide them. They paid brokers out of their own pockets and recovered the money a little at a time from the annual 12b-1 fee they charged. Just to make sure that you didn't bail out of the fund before you'd ponied up all the money, they tacked on a surrender fee that declined over six or seven years.

Most broker-sold fund groups followed this trend, creating two classes of mutual fund shares. The A shares carried the traditional sales commission that investors paid up-front. The B shares substituted an annual 12b-1 fee and a surrender fee for the up-front load.

In July 1992, the National Association of

Securities Dealers capped the 12b-1 at .75 percent to recover the sales commission and another .25 percent as a broker's service fee.

The cost is only half the story. Studies show that these fees can force portfolio managers to take on more risk. A 1995 bond fund study by Morningstar Mutual Funds found that portfolio managers saddled with the high annual expenses of B shares took on additional investment risk in an effort to match the performance of funds with lower expenses.

Morningstar broke the bond fund universe into two camps: those with 12b-1 fees and those without. The first group had an average expense ratio of 1.10 percent; the second, .64 percent. Some quick math shows that if the managers all held the same bonds, the funds with B shares would return .46 percent less. But there was almost no difference between the returns, as the chart below shows.

The managers of funds with B shares took on much more risk—measured by a higher **STANDARD DEVIATION**—in order to compete with managers who enjoyed low expenses. In 1994, when the bond market went in the tank, that risk boomeranged. Bond funds with no B expenses lost 3.78 percent. Those with B fees dropped 5.27 percent. And those with B fees of .75 percent or more lost 6.4 percent.

180

RETURN ON LOAD FUNDS		
ANNUALIZED RETURN	B SHARES	W/O 12B-I FEES
3-year	5.22%	5.45%
5-year	7.43%	7.50%
10-year	8.54%	8.54%

DO start with just one fund if that's all you can afford.

A portfolio or group of three or more funds is ideal. But starting with just one fund is much better than keeping your money in the bank. Don't be intimidated by the suggestion that you must be an investment pro with lots of money to invest.

◆ Think of your single fund as the core of what will someday be a group of funds.

◆ Buy a fund that's a proven winner. Don't experiment.

◆ If you can't come up with the minimum initial deposit, find a fund that will waive the minimum if you make regular, systematic deposits from your paycheck or bank account.

◆ Plan to buy and hold. You should think of investing as a long-term program.

Here are some funds for a "starter kit":

Balanced Funds These funds invest in both the stock and bond markets. Some require a mix of, say, 60 percent stocks and 40 percent bonds. Others give their managers more leeway. But all balanced funds invest in both markets, which makes their returns less volatile. It also keeps these returns somewhat lower than a pure stock fund's.

An excellent choice is the Vanguard/Wellington fund. This veteran, set up in July 1929, returned an average of 7.8 percent a year from inception through the end of 1994. That compares with an **AVERAGE ANNUAL RETURN** of 9.2 percent for the Standard & Poor's 500

AVERAGE ANNUAL RETURN *The average return of a fund for each year over a period of years.*

Stock Index and 5.4 percent for bonds, as measured by the Salomon Brothers High-Grade Bond Index for the period. So the fund has done just what it set out to do: provide balance.

Index Funds Index funds contain a mix of securities that mimics a market index such as the Standard & Poor's 500. Because such a fund holds securities in the same relative weightings as the index and trades infrequently, expenses are low. In a good index fund, returns parallel the market. Index funds work well for beginners because there is no portfolio manager to monitor.

The best index fund, hands down, is the Vanguard Index 500 Trust, set up in 1976. The fund charges about 20 basis points—or $^2/_{10}$ of a percentage point—in expenses, compared with 1.33 percent for the average stock fund. Although the fund is huge—over $18 billion in assets—size is not a problem. The money simply goes into the stocks that make up the index. Thanks to its efficiencies and low costs, this fund has done an excellent job of following the market.

Equity Income Funds These are among the most conservative of stock fund offerings. Good choices include Fidelity Equity-Income II, Hotchkis & Wiley Equity-Income, and T. Rowe Price Equity-Income.

Finally, here is an unusual choice: SoGen International is a global **ASSET ALLOCATION** fund, which provides exposure to all types of assets all over the world in a single fund. As a category, asset allocation funds are not good performers. This fund is an exception to the rule and well worth considering as the basis of a one-fund portfolio.

32

DON'T invest in a fund that's too big for its britches.

Because brand names matter to consumers when they buy refrigerators or computers, many mutual fund companies have attempted to market brand-name mutual funds. A name means much less in mutual fund investing. Some of the better-known funds with household names have left their glory days behind them, chiefly because they've grown too large. Managing a big stock fund is like turning an ocean liner as opposed to a sailboat.

The best example is the biggest: Fidelity Magellan, which tops $50 billion in assets. Many investors still buy Magellan because of the record set by Peter Lynch, the portfolio manager with the best 10-year record in mutual fund history. In fact, the fund has had two managers since Lynch left in 1990, and it has a much different style today. A software program from BARRA, a research firm, shows that in 1979, with Lynch at the helm, 80 percent of the fund was invested in small-company growth stocks and 20 percent in large-company growth. In 1994, just 20 percent was in small-company growth, 20 percent in large-company growth, and 60 in large-company value stocks. Small-company stocks have much more growth potential than large-company stocks.

Jeffrey Vinik, who has been in charge since 1992, has done a brilliant job with Magellan. But his fund is far more concentrated—500 stocks, down from 1,200 under Lynch. And Vinik makes huge **SECTOR BETS**, while Lynch's choices were spread broadly across the market.

Fidelity's name and marketing pizzazz can

113

draw millions of dollars into a fund in the blink of an eye. Fidelity Asset Manager accumulated $10.9 billion in its first five years—but it failed to beat the market in both 1994 and 1995, losing 6.6 percent in 1994 and gaining only half as much as the market in 1995.

A better indication that a fund is doing a good job is the decision to close to new investors when there is too much money to invest wisely. Consider FPA Paramount, a growth-and-income fund that closed in 1984 when it reached $100 million, opened for nine weeks in 1989, and closed again until fall 1994, when it opened for six months and reached $500 million in assets. Manager William Sams doesn't believe he can get good returns unless he keeps the fund at a manageable size.

Size isn't so important for bond funds or balanced funds. And it isn't a problem for index funds like the Vanguard Index 500. But non-index stock funds require a nimble manager.

THE TEN LARGEST STOCK FUNDS

STOCK FUND	ASSETS	1995 PERFORMANCE
Fidelity Magellan	$53.8 billion	36.82
Investment Co. of America	25.26	30.63
Washington Mutual Investors	18.06	41.22
Vanguard Index 500	16.55	37.45
20th Century Ultra	14.78	37.68
Fidelity Contrafund	14.49	36.28
Fidelity Growth & Income	14.04	35.38
Vanguard/Windsor	13.73	30.15
Janus	12.38	29.43
Fidelity Equity-Income II	11.55	26.39
Standard & Poor's 500	—	37.53

DO take a skeptical attitude toward mutual fund ratings.

Investors are often told to consider only those funds that have received a four-star or five-star rating—such as Franklin Small-Cap Growth, Putnam New Opportunities, or Robertson Stephens Value+Growth—from Morningstar Mutual Funds. The problem is this: the rationale behind the star ratings relies almost entirely on recent past performance. For example, Fidelity Select Biotechnology had no stars at its trough and five stars at its peak.

The ratings were never intended to be predictive, says Don Phillips, president of Morningstar. "We're the first to concede the limitations of the star ratings," Phillips says. "We label it as a historical profile. It's 100 percent accurate in measuring past performance." In the case of Fidelity Select Biotechnology, it makes perfect sense that when the fund was new, it had no track record and no stars. When the fund established a great track record, it had five stars.

Phillips compares the star system to baseball batting averages; on opening day, everyone starts with zero. "If you have a player who goes four for four on opening day, he starts the day with an average of zero and ends the day with a 1.000," Phillips says. "When it's zero, you know he's not going to go the whole season without getting a hit. At the end of opening day, you don't expect him to bat 1.000 all year."

The ratings can be useful to investors who use them as one piece of information. But they are not a security blanket, as investors in

Fidelity Asset Manager learned in 1994. That fund had a five-star rating for all of 1993 and 1994. But by the end of 1994, it had lost 6.6 percent.

Here are some tips for evaluating a fund:

◆ Check the fund's history. The ratings are most helpful for diversified funds—like Dodge & Cox Stock or Mutual Shares—with a long history under the same manager.

◆ Disregard ratings for **SECTOR FUNDS** like Fidelity Select Biotechnology. Here the ratings depict the recent popularity of that sector as much as the manager's ability. If the sector has been hot in the recent past, it may be set for a cooldown.

206

◆ Be careful of ratings for aggressive growth funds like the Kaufmann Fund and Twentieth Century Giftrust, which can be volatile performers. Look at the annual returns for each year over the past decade to see if you can handle the potential losses.

◆ Check to see how long the fund has been rated and its average score. For example, Sequoia has an average rating of 4.9 stars over 10 years.

◆ Read the **MORNINGSTAR ANALYSIS** carefully. You will learn, for example, that the two managers of the Kaufmann Fund "short stocks," or borrow stock and sell it, believing that the price will go down so that they can buy the stock at a lower price and repay the loan, making a profit. This is a high-risk strategy.

212

◆ Look to see if the fund has grown dramatically in size. For example, assets in PBHG Growth exploded when the company removed the fund's load in 1993. Rapidly growing assets can make it difficult for a manager to hold to his strategy.

DON'T pay attention to what a fund calls itself.

What's in a fund name? Is Fidelity Balanced a balanced fund? How about Fidelity Growth & Income? Investing in different types of funds with different objectives is an important investment goal. But selecting a fund based on its name is a big mistake.

There are two problems with using names for guidance. First, some fund companies attempt to maneuver their funds into a category in which they will achieve better performance than the rest of the group. For example, I might name my aggressive growth fund Rowland Growth & Income. If my aggressive strategy works, I should outperform the more conservative growth-and-income funds. But the name conceals the risks I'm taking—and you're taking them along with me.

Other misleading names are the product of the funds' marketing departments. If you wanted to sell a fund, would you call it XYZ High Risk? Probably not. XYZ Conservative Growth has a much better ring, doesn't it? Solid, yet on the prowl for growth. But the name is designed to soothe and woo investors rather than give them information about the fund's objective.

If you were thumbing through the mutual fund tables looking for a large-cap growth fund, you might think that Fidelity Blue Chip Growth would be just the ticket. How wrong you would be! Fidelity, the supreme marketer

---

INITIAL PUBLIC OFFERING *The first time the stock of a company is offered to the public.*

in this business, has a habit of giving funds catchy names and then allowing portfolio managers to do just about whatever they want with them, often with good—albeit unpredictable—results.

This is what Morningstar analyst Amy C. Arnott has said about Fidelity Blue Chip: "When manager Michael Gordon took over in early 1993, he didn't hesitate to get rid of the blue-chip stalwarts that had dominated the portfolio in the past. In their stead, he loaded up on small and medium-size stocks, slicing the portfolio's median market cap to a fifth of its former size." Market cap, of course, refers to the average size of the companies in the portfolio. Large-cap stocks are companies with market values (total shares outstanding multiplied by current stock price) of more than $10 billion; small-caps are generally companies with market values of less than $500 million; mid-caps are somewhere in between.

Arnott also said that this shouldn't come as a surprise, given the fact that Gordon started his career as an analyst of **INITIAL PUBLIC OFFERINGS** (IPOs), private companies that are being offered to the market for the first time. He also loaded up on foreign securities. Therefore, investors in search of a core holding in blue-chip growth stocks should look elsewhere.

That does not mean that Fidelity Blue Chip is not a good fund. But it does mean that the niche it fills in your portfolio is the medium-cap-growth rather than the large-cap-growth stock slot. Diversifying your portfolio requires a clear understanding of the role each fund plays. That information cannot be gleaned from its name.

DO use index funds.

O.K., it's not glamorous to be average. But only about one quarter of portfolio managers beat the market in a given year. And they're not always the same ones. The argument for matching the market is compelling, even if it is not exciting. Most managers fail to beat the market because the costs of trading, administration, and other fees eat into returns. Expenses for the average managed stock fund total 1.33 percent a year. An index fund minimizes trading, eliminates management fees, and reduces other costs of doing business by simply putting together a basket of the same stocks that make up the overall market index. The investor who buys an index fund duplicates the market's performance at a low cost.

Institutional investors, such as pension funds, pour billions into low-cost index funds. But retail customers came around to them slowly. John C. Bogle, chairman of the Vanguard Group, introduced the first index fund for individuals in 1976. That fund, the Vanguard Index 500, duplicates the Standard & Poor's 500 index (see graph). When Vanguard opened the fund, the expense ratio was 45 basis points, or less than $\frac{1}{2}$ of 1 percent of assets under management. By 1995, expenses had dropped to just 19 basis points. The Vanguard Index 500 tracks the S&P, just slightly underperforming due to the fund's expenses.

Be wary of index funds that add some fancy twist that detracts from performance and hikes

WILSHIRE 5000 *An index of all stocks traded on all exchanges in the U.S. (There are actually more than 6,000 today.)*

expenses. Some of them even carry loads. Vanguard, too, expanded on the idea, adding funds that follow other indexes. For example, the Vanguard Index Total Stock Market attempts to replicate the performance of the **WILSHIRE 5000**. The Vanguard Index Extended Market buys stocks in the Wilshire 4500, which is the Wilshire 5000 minus the S&P 500, and the Vanguard Index Small-Cap Stock fund seeks to replicate returns of the **RUSSELL 2000**. Vanguard also offers overseas index funds.

42 ▶

Small-cap and overseas markets are less efficient than the large-cap arena of the S&P 500. A good manager *can* add value by stock picking. But if you are an investor who does not want to monitor investments, this is the best way to set up an all-stock portfolio:

50% Vanguard Index 500 Trust
25% Vanguard Index Small-Cap Stock
25% split between Vanguard International Equity Index European and Vanguard International Equity Index Pacific

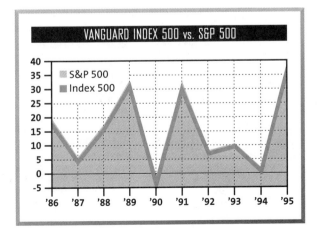

VANGUARD INDEX 500 vs. S&P 500

■ S&P 500
■ Index 500

DON'T try to time the market.

The market goes up and down in sudden spurts. But the long-term direction is up. You can stay invested and ride along the upward (sometimes rocky) path, or you can stay on the sidelines and lose out on much of the long-term return.

Stocks often lose out to bonds or money market instruments in the short term. Consider the year-by-year comparison from 1960 to 1995 in the chart at right.

As you can see, the market's pattern is unpredictable. Market timers use various types of technical analyses to examine trends and look for patterns in the market. For example, many consider the movement of small investors into the market to be a signal that it's time to get out. But as you know if you read *The Wall Street Journal* or other business publications, these timers are often predicting doomsday while the market marches merrily ahead.

Just when things seem gloomiest—as they did in 1973 and 1974—the market takes off. And sometimes, when market timers are predicting a correction, it seems like the good times roll on forever—or almost—as they did during the 1980s.

At the end of 1994, when stocks finished the year with a gain of just over 1 percent, financial advisers said they fielded dozens of calls from clients asking if they should get out of stocks. Then, in 1995, the market exploded in one of its most spectacular rallies in history, up 37.5 percent for the year. "I'd love to be chatting with the market timers now," says Deena Katz, a financial planner in Coral Gables, Fla.

RETURNS ON STOCKS AND BONDS

YEAR	STOCKS	BONDS	T-BILLS
1960	0.5	11.8	2.7
1961	26.9	1.8	2.1
1962	−8.7	5.6	2.7
1963	22.8	1.6	3.1
1964	16.5	4.0	3.5
1965	12.5	1.0	3.9
1966	−10.1	4.7	4.8
1967	24.0	1.0	4.2
1968	11.1	4.5	5.2
1969	−8.5	−0.7	6.6
1970	4.0	16.9	6.5
1971	14.3	8.7	4.4
1972	19.0	5.2	3.8
1973	−14.7	4.6	6.9
1974	−26.5	5.7	8.0
1975	37.2	7.8	5.8
1976	23.8	12.9	5.1
1977	−7.2	1.4	5.1
1978	6.6	3.5	7.2
1979	18.4	4.1	10.4
1980	32.4	3.9	11.2
1981	−4.9	9.5	14.7
1982	21.4	29.1	10.5
1983	22.5	7.4	8.8
1984	6.3	14.0	9.8
1985	32.2	20.3	7.7
1986	18.5	15.1	6.2
1987	5.2	2.9	5.5
1988	16.8	6.1	6.3
1989	31.5	13.3	8.4
1990	−3.2	9.7	7.8
1991	30.5	15.5	5.6
1992	7.7	7.2	3.5
1993	10.0	11.2	2.9
1994	1.3	−3.5	3.9
1995	37.5	30.0	3.8

Source: Ibbotson Associates and Sanford C. Bernstein

DO invest in different asset classes.

ASSET allocation—selecting the right mix of asset classes, such as international stocks, small-company stocks, large-company stocks—determines an astounding 90 percent of your return, while selecting the right stock or mutual fund accounts for just 10 percent, according to many studies.

Not surprisingly, asset allocation has become the buzzword in investing. But what does it really mean? Simply that you should include a broad range of funds in your portfolio.

Many investors consider just three asset classes: stocks, bonds, and cash. That's too narrow. You should invest in different types of stock funds, including those that invest for value, those that invest for growth, those that buy small companies, those that buy large companies, and those that invest overseas.

Here are some asset classes, all of which are represented by mutual funds:

Cash Equivalents
- money market funds and Treasury bills

Bonds
- short-term bonds (3- to 5-year maturities)
- intermediate-term bonds (5- to 10-year maturities)

U.S. Small-Company Stocks
- growth
- value
- micro (invests in tiny companies)

ASSETS *Anything of value. In discussing investments, the term usually refers to the amount of money you have to invest or to the amount of money a mutual fund manager has in a fund.*

U.S. Large-Company Stocks
◆ core, like the S&P 500 Stock Index
◆ growth
◆ value
◆ yield, such as an equity income fund

International
◆ developed countries
◆ emerging markets

Inflation Hedges
◆ natural resources funds
◆ real estate funds
◆ energy funds

Specialty
◆ sector funds

For most investors, stocks should represent the bulk of their portfolio. How much? Many portfolio managers invest 100 percent of their personal portfolios in stocks. But some studies show there is little to be gained with the final 15 percent. In other words, a long-term portfolio that is 85 percent stocks and 15 percent short-term bonds or cash might be ideal in that it provides stock market returns with a small cushion against stock market volatility.

The 85 percent that is in stocks should be spread across the stock groups listed above. Some investors neglect to put money into large, established U.S. companies because they rightly believe that the real growth will come from small, undiscovered companies or from those companies just getting established in developing countries. But investors who pursued that strategy in 1995 were sorely disappointed. Large-company U.S. stocks raced ahead, gaining more than 37 percent and leaving small-company, international, and emerging markets in the dust. Make certain that you are covered in all these categories.

DON'T buy asset allocation funds for your portfolio.

You need asset allocation, right? Then why not get someone to do it for you? It's but another gimmick. When the stock market crashed in October 1987, mutual fund marketers frantically searched for a way to keep investors from heading for the exits. This was their thinking: Investors are afraid of the stock market. Why not promote funds that "allocate" their assets among a variety of types of securities, cushioning them from big swings in any single market?

One of the most pretentious of the early offerings was the National Securities Strategic Allocation Fund. Four times a year, a group of money managers from around the world met in a town house on Manhattan's Upper East Side to discuss the international economy and decide how to allocate the assets in the fund.

"This particular fund," said Andre Sharon, the fund's "allocator," at a meeting in March 1988, "represents the ideal way of managing money by looking at the whole world as your potential oyster, folding in and out of different sectors when you feel the relative real rates of return will favor one sector over another."

I went to one of these meetings and watched the five market specialists plus Sharon sip coffee and orange juice and munch on croissants while they discussed the pros and cons of, say, precious **METALS** versus foreign stocks. Not surprisingly, each specialist liked the outlook for his own sector. I left feeling I wouldn't want my money drifting around the world based on the whims of this group. Not only does this mumbo jumbo result in high expenses, but all that asset shifting makes the fund a market timer and, eventually, a failure.

In the first quarter of 1988, the fund gained 2.47 percent versus 6.6 percent for the S&P. It no longer exists.

Asset allocation funds have these problems:

◆ They cannot really be categorized. One fund might be all in cash; another might invest its money in other mutual funds. That means you don't know what you're getting. It's difficult to compare returns of apples and oranges.

◆ Performance is poor. In 1994, a disastrous year in the stock and bond markets, the average asset allocation fund did worse than both market averages, with a loss of 3.05 percent, according to Morningstar Mutual Funds. That compared with a gain of 1.32 percent for the S&P 500, a loss of 2.66 for the Wilshire 5000 Index, and a loss of 2.92 for the Lehman Brothers Aggregate Bond Index.

◆ A soothing name can hide a lot of sins. Consider Fidelity Asset Manager, one of the fastest-growing funds in history, out of the gate in 1988 and up to $12 billion in assets at the end of 1994. As it turned out, the fund was allocating its assets to very aggressive investments in '94, with 8 percent in derivatives tied to foreign interest rates and commodities, and nearly half in foreign securities, including 17 percent in Mexico when the peso crashed. The fund lost 6.6 percent for the year.

The exception that proves the rule: SoGen International, a global asset allocation fund run by Jean-Marie Eveillard, a portfolio manager worth his fee. This established fund provides exposure to markets around the world and brings you the management of Eveillard, who is unique in his ability to provide good performance and low risk.

DO manage your own cash.

Avoid stock funds with large holdings (more than 10 percent of assets) in cash. Some managers move into cash when they believe the markets are heading down. You should look for a manager who stays invested. You are paying a manager to invest for you, not to sit on the sidelines and charge you big bucks for doing nothing. Or to frenetically move money among cash, stocks, bonds, and so forth. Investment pros are no better at timing the market than you are. Frequent trading also runs up transaction costs and generates taxes.

A large cash position does not always mean the manager is timing the market. It's possible that a manager has accumulated a lot of cash because the fund suddenly became very popular and he can't find enough good investments for the inflows. In that case, perhaps he should consider closing the fund. Either way, it's not a good time for you to invest in that fund.

A 1995 Morningstar study found that funds with large cash positions underperformed funds with small cash positions. The study compared funds that stayed fully invested with those that sometimes used a cash cushion and those that timed the market by moving large amounts of assets into and out of cash.

The results were clear-cut: the two extremes did the worst. The funds that never had money in cash had an average annual return of 8.26 percent over a five-year period. Those that timed the market by moving 50 percent or more of assets into cash did somewhat worse, with 8.25 percent annual return over five years. The most reliable performers were those in the group that altered their cash positions by less than 15 percent, which is the group you should be looking at. Average annual returns here were 9.04 percent over five years. Equally significant, even the worst performers in this group showed positive returns.

The best performers were those that sometimes raised cash—15 to 25 percent of the fund—with an average annual return of 9.58 percent over five years. The problem with this group, though, is that it also included a number of losers. "Although funds using flexible approaches to cash had the best overall total returns, it's clear that this **INVESTMENT STYLE** still supplies plenty of rope for funds to hang themselves with," wrote Jeff Kelley, a Morningstar analyst.

110

Further, the more cash funds used, the greater the disparity in their performance. Many of the worst performers in the group that used more than 35 percent cash had negative returns. "The wider a fund's cash range, the greater the amount of disappointment it can deliver," Kelley said.

To find out how a fund uses cash, read the reports the fund sends. The manager may say that he is "defensive" because he thinks the market is too high and is selling securities and raising cash. You could also call the company and ask if the fund always stays fully invested. Or check the Morningstar analysis. Consider Crabbe Huson Equity, a fund that trounced the competition in 1991, '92, and '93. By 1995, comanagers Dick Huson and Jahn Maack had grown cautious and resisted investing the incoming cash stream. Cash ranged between 20 percent and 35 percent of assets, according to Morningstar. Of course, the market soared, and the fund did not fully share in those gains.

DON'T buy and sell with your emotions.

People often write to me for investing advice. Most of them have made the same mistake: investing on impulse. Some of them choose a fund because it's a household name. Some buy one when they read that it's about to close or because it was the No. 1 performer over the past year. Some lose money and vow never to invest again. For all of them, the solution I offer is the same: choose an investment dispassionately and then stick with it. Discipline—not picking the best performer—is the key to investment success.

Rocky markets with lots of economic uncertainty can shake even the most disciplined investors. If you know that you will be tested by such periods, you can resolve not to make the mistake of jumping ship. Consider the period of July 1990 through March 1991. These nine months were a time of great investor fears fed by recession, massive layoffs, the Persian Gulf war, and uncertainty in the insurance industry because of the failure of Executive Life, a major insurer.

The benefits-consulting firm of Foster Higgins in Princeton, N.J., did a survey of 50 employers in March 1991, asking them if employees had responded to these troubling events by altering the investments in their 401(k) plans. They had. Most of them fled to

MONEY MARKET FUND *Invests in short-term debt instruments such as high-quality corporate commercial paper and Treasury securities. Because it maintains a stable share price, a money market fund is considered the safest type of mutual fund.*

safety, moving out of the stock market and into "safe" investments like a **MONEY MARKET FUND**. As it happens, though, investors who moved out of equities did so at the stock market trough in August 1990. The market rebounded quickly, showing one of its strongest rallies in the fall of 1990 and winter of 1991. "The majority of transfers were out of stocks and into fixed-income funds," said Richard J. Knapp, who was then a principal at Foster Higgins. "People are shifting their money in the wrong direction. They are buying high and selling low."

The year 1994 was another testing ground for investors. Bonds turned in one of their worst years in history, and stocks, as measured by the Standard & Poor's 500 Stock Index, gained a measly 1.32 percent. But investors who got discouraged and pulled out of the markets missed the spectacular rally of 1995.

Successful investing is just the opposite of buying and selling on whim. Never buy on the spur of the moment. Never buy the "hot" fund. Never sell because the market drops.

Instead

◆ Compile a list of funds that interest you. Gather information about each one. Call the companies and ask questions about the funds.

◆ Invest with a plan in mind. Five years should be your minimum time horizon; 10 years is better.

◆ Decide before you invest what conditions would prompt a sale. For example, the portfolio manager leaves, the fund requests changes in investment strategy, it grows too large, or it consistently lags behind its peers (other funds with the same investment objectives). Otherwise, sit tight.

DO look under the hood.

Make sure any funds you're considering (and the ones you already own) follow their investment objectives. If you take the trouble to select a fund that will use a value approach to picking small-company stocks, you want to be certain that that's what the manager does.

Many funds drift from their stated objectives to wherever the best current returns are. Over the past couple of years, fund companies have requested changes in investment policy to give managers broad powers to go wherever they think they can make some money. This is usually bad news for investors. You may believe you have carefully diversified your **PORTFOLIO** only to find that funds of every stripe have selected the same high-flying company or **SECTOR**. Only when the hot stock or industry runs into trouble do you discover that you were overexposed.

Many U.S. funds are increasing their bets overseas to goose returns. If you selected just one fund and you wanted the manager to go wherever the best returns were, that would be fine. You might choose Templeton Growth or SoGen International.

But if you picked one fund to invest in small U.S. companies and another to invest in emerging overseas markets, you do not want both funds to buy the same overseas stock. Consider what happened when the peso crashed in the spring of 1995. Investors who owned the Scudder Latin America fund were

PORTFOLIO *A collection of investments, which might include stocks, bonds, gold, art, and real estate.*

probably not surprised that Teléfonos de México was its largest holding. But what of the many Fidelity domestic-stock funds and other U.S. funds that bought the same stock, giving many investors much more exposure to that company than they suspected?

Consider Acorn, a small-company fund with 12.5 percent of assets in **EMERGING MARKETS**. Or Lindner Growth, a U.S. growth fund with 32 percent overseas. Or Warburg Pincus Growth & Income, a fund with no income and a 22 percent stake in precious metals.

74

These funds were used as examples because they are all top-rated high performers. That can serve to lull shareholders to sleep. They might wake up when they find out what the portfolio manager has been doing to get the returns. For example, Warburg Pincus Growth & Income, with a five-star Morningstar rating, racked up great returns in the early '90s. Happy investors might not have noticed that it produced almost no income, which is, after all, one of the objectives of the growth-and-income group.

Further, because portfolio manager Anthony Orphanos believed gold was on its way to $800 an ounce, he stocked up on precious-metals stocks. Whether Orphanos was right or wrong, gold is hardly the investment of choice for a growth-and-income fund. It provides no growth and no income.

This does not mean that you should never consider one of these funds. But if you choose one, you should know that the manager plans to take a flexible approach to investing your money. That means more work in putting together your portfolio to make certain there isn't too much overlap with your other funds.

DON'T buy (or sell) a fund based on recent performance alone.

Personal finance magazines tout the top-performing fund of the past year—or even quarter. That's not the time for you to buy into it. And it's not time to sell a fund you hold just because it appears on the list of worst performers. Investments are cyclical. If you overemphasize recent past performance, you may be buying funds at the peak. And you may be selling funds that are poised to do well.

Your task as an investor is to set up a portfolio that will do well in all types of market climates. That does not mean each of your funds will be a top performer every quarter. You want funds that complement one another and that perform well in different environments. Sometimes the market favors growth funds, sometimes value funds. Sometimes small-company stocks have a big run, and sometimes the large-cap stocks, like those in the S&P 500 index, outpace everything else in the market. Overseas stocks, too, have their cycles. All of these asset classes together should create a portfolio that weathers most storms.

A good fund is one that sticks to its knitting. When its style goes temporarily out of favor, that fund underperforms. If you think about it, that's as it should be. You don't want a manager who suddenly changes his style to go where the returns are. You've picked him to do what he's good at and to fulfill a specific

CONTRARIAN *A style in which investors buy what is currently out of favor in the market, reasoning that it offers good value because the price is low and that it will come back into favor.*

role in your portfolio. Consider the Mutual Series funds managed by Michael Price, one of the best-known **VALUE INVESTORS**. In 1987, when the stock market crashed, Price did just fine. And in 1988, his performance was terrific. Investors who bought that two-year record were probably sorry in the following three years, when value investing fell out of favor. Those who threw in the towel would be sorrier still as Price got back on track. A **CONTRARIAN** investor would probably have bought Mutual Beacon in 1991, reasoning that it was time for a turnaround in value investing.

Look at Price's returns for Mutual Beacon compared with the market in the chart below. Notice that the only year Price actually lost money was 1990. But he underperformed the market for three years running. Still, investors who bought the fund in 1989 because of his recent record and sold after the 1990 loss would have been disappointed, with good reason. Unfortunately, that's exactly what many investors do.

110

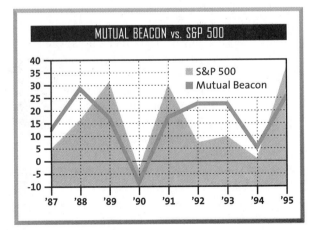

MUTUAL BEACON vs. S&P 500

■ S&P 500
■ Mutual Beacon

DO look for consistency.

You want a fund that does what you expect it to do and does it repeatedly, finishing in the top half among funds in its category at least four years out of five. Avoid funds that perform erratically (top quartile one year, bottom the next) compared with their peers, even if their long-term performance is above average.

Thomas R. Ebright, comanager of the Pennsylvania Mutual Fund, often compares building a mutual fund portfolio to building a baseball team. "You want players who will work together, complement each others' strengths, and cover each others' weaknesses; players who are consistent hitters, and a couple of defensive stars as well," he says. Ebright suggests that you assemble a team of 6 to 10 players and patiently stick with them, even though each has an occasional off season.

Unfortunately, Ebright's own fund lacks consistency. Ebright and Charles M. Royce buy small-company stocks, which are subject to extreme market cycles. Historically, small stocks have outperformed larger stocks, a fact that gives them an important place in an investor's portfolio. But they can also languish for long periods, as they did for much of the 1980s. During those years, Pennsylvania Mutual was considered one of the top small-company funds, appearing often on "model portfolio" lists. Look at how it performed compared with the S&P 500 and the **RUSSELL 2000** (see

RUSSELL 2000 *An index of 2,000 small-cap stocks. The average market capitalization for small-cap companies at the end of 1994 was $211 million.*

graph). Notice that the only year Pennsylvania Mutual lost money was 1990, which was the turnaround year for small-company stocks. It underperformed the S&P consistently over the last half of the '80s, which is exactly what you would expect of a small-company fund when big-company stocks are doing well. It generally outperformed the Russell 2000 index, yet it was hardly consistent. By 1990, even a patient investor might have begun to question it .

Look, though, at what happened to Penn Mutual when small-company stocks rallied. Although it did well, it didn't keep up with the Russell index. It was inconsistent, underperforming the small-cap index during three years of a strong rally. Part of the reason is that it holds so many stocks—300 to 500. Even Royce and Ebright seem to have felt something new was necessary: in 1991, they introduced Royce Micro-Cap, which invests in tiny companies, and Royce Premier, which skims the best companies from Pennsylvania Mutual. Both racked up strong three-year records.

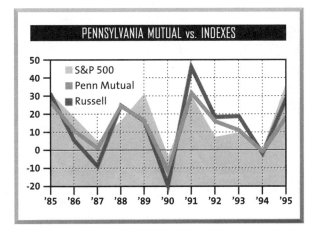

DON'T buy a fund with high turnover.

Fund managers have various investment styles. Some trade heavily and frequently. Others spend a great deal of time on research, buy a select few companies, and stick with them for the long term. Consider Longleaf Partners Fund, managed by O. Mason Hawkins and G. Staley Cates. The two have all their own money invested in the fund, and they take the research seriously, visiting companies they buy, talking to management, and evaluating the prospects. They concentrate on the 20 or 30 best companies they can find and then buy to hold. All of these characteristics make a fund a good long-term investment with a low **PORTFOLIO TURNOVER RATE**. Other funds—particularly small-cap growth funds—might trade every security in the portfolio in a year, or even twice in a year.

Transaction costs and taxes in a fund with a high turnover can drain returns. Every time the manager sells a security at a profit, you have both additional transaction charges and a **CAPITAL GAINS** tax liability. A 1995 study by Sanford C. Bernstein & Co. looked at the effect of turnover on returns. Here are the assumptions: state and local tax rates of 40 percent on income and 32 percent on capital gains; 10 percent a year average return on a stock portfolio over 20 years. Bernstein assumed that after 20 years, the investor

66

PORTFOLIO TURNOVER RATE *Refers to the percentage of the portfolio that is bought and sold each year. A turnover rate of 50 percent means half the securities are exchanged in a year.*

liquidated the portfolio and paid all taxes.

If the portfolio has an annual turnover of 25 percent—in other words, one quarter of the securities are bought and sold each year—it will compound at 6.64 percent a year after transaction costs and taxes. If half the portfolio turns over, the compounding rate drops to 6.3 percent. If the entire portfolio is traded each year, at least some of the gains will be short term and therefore taxed at a higher rate. If the portfolio turns over twice a year, with all the gains short term, the return shrinks to 4.66 percent a year. (Check the prospectus.)

Although the percentages seem small, their impact is huge over a long period (see chart). To overcome the big drop in return, a high-turnover fund must earn a great deal more. For example, if the portfolio is turned over at 200 percent a year, it must compound at 13.36 percent before taxes and commissions to net the same after-tax return as a portfolio that earns 10 percent with a 25 percent turnover.

HOW TURNOVER AFFECTS NET RETURN

PORTFOLIO MANAGER	GROSS RETURN	% TURNOVER	RETURN* AFTER COSTS	$5 MILL AFTER 20 YRS	% GROSS REVENUE MATCH
A	10	25	6.64	$18.1	—
B	10	50	6.30	17.0	10.48
C	10	100	5.66	15.0	11.50
D	10	150	5.20	13.8	12.28
E	10	200	4.66	12.4	13.36

Assumes all taxes are paid after 20 years; 40% aggregate income taxes; 32% aggregate capital gains tax; one quarter of gains taken at 100 percent turnover are short-term as are half the gains at 150% and all gains at 200 percent. Portfolio is liquidated after 20 years, and all taxes are paid.

SOURCE: SANFORD C. BERNSTEIN

DO buy funds from a single family or a discount broker.

Fees are important. Avoiding them is getting trickier. The cheapest way to set up a portfolio is to use a single fund family or to use a discount brokerage that offers funds from a number of fund groups at no transaction cost. The most popular program is Charles Schwab's OneSource, or no transaction fee, program. Jack White & Co. and Fidelity FundsNetwork also offer no-fee programs.

In addition to cutting fees, using a single family or a discount broker makes record keeping much simpler. If you have funds at a number of fund families and you receive reports from each of them, it is very difficult to evaluate the performance of your portfolio or to move money from one fund to another to rebalance your portfolio. That's why most financial planners move their clients' accounts to a discount broker like Schwab. "When a new client comes in with all these bits of paper from different fund companies and brokers, the first thing I do is move everything to Schwab," says H. Lynn Hopewell, a planner in Falls Church, Va. If you are a novice investor, it might seem intimidating to be faced with so many choices—more than 900 funds are available through Schwab and even more through Jack White. But help is available.

In a report on single-family investing, Sheldon Jacobs, editor of *The No-Load Fund Investor,* set up three model portfolios at each of six no-load fund groups: Fidelity, Vanguard, T. Rowe Price, Invesco, Scudder, and Strong. You can get the report, which includes model portfolios from Fidelity FundsNetwork and Charles

Schwab's OneSource, by sending $1 to *The No-Load Fund Investor,* P.O. Box 318, Irvington-on-Hudson, N.Y. 10533.

For beginning investors who want to stick with one family, T. Rowe Price is a particularly good choice because it offers solid funds in every category as well as top-notch shareholder information and communications. The chart below shows two of Jacobs's three model port-folios using all Price funds. His third portfolio, which is designed for retirees, modifies the preretirement portfolio by decreasing domes-tic and foreign stock investments and increas-ing the percent in Spectrum Income, a fund composed of seven other Price funds, to 35 percent. A buy-and-hold investor could do very well with these portfolios without ever moving to another fund company.

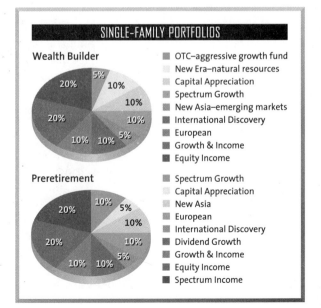

DON'T ignore expenses.

All funds charge expenses. But these charges vary widely. Paying attention to them is critical. Over the long term, expenses have a major impact on investment returns. Here are some of the expenses charged by mutual funds.

Loads A load is a sales charge that typically goes to pay the broker who sells the fund. However, some funds that are sold directly over the phone, most notably many of those at Fidelity Investments, also impose loads. A front-end load is subtracted from your money before it is invested. A back-end load, deferred sales charge, and redemption fee all mean the same thing—that a fee is deducted when you are ready to take your money out.

16

12b-1 Fees RULE 12B-1, approved in October 1980 by the SEC, allows funds to charge for marketing and distribution costs. The fee might range from .25 percent to 1 percent. This money comes out of the fund year after year. The National Association of Securities Dealers limits funds sold by its members to a 12b-1 fee of no more than .75 percent plus a servicing fee of .25 percent, or 25 **BASIS POINTS**, for a total of 1 percent.

Other expenses include management fees to pay the portfolio manager, certain administrative expenses, and fees to exchange shares from one fund to another.

Some expenses, like management salaries and administrative expenses, cannot be avoided. But you should be looking for funds with

BASIS POINT *$1/100$ of 1 percent. It is used to measure such things as expenses and yields.*

no load, no 12b-1 fee, and low expenses—
under 75 basis points. A 1988 ruling by the
SEC made it easier for investors to figure out
how much a fund charges in fees. The fund
must identify all fees in the prospectus as well
as demonstrate how they would affect a $1,000
investment that earns a hypothetical 5 percent
after 1 year, 3 years, 5 years, and 10 years.

Consider the example below from the Scudder Value fund. The total expenses charged by
this fund amount to 1.25 percent of the assets
per year, compared with an average of 1.33
percent a year for a diversified equity fund.
However, notice the asterisk? This prospectus
contains a footnote indicating that Scudder
has promised to hold expenses at 1.25 percent
until Jan. 1, 1996. Actual expenses for the fund
during the period were 1.61 percent. In January, Scudder extended the period that expenses would be "capped" until July 31, 1996.

Shareholder Transaction Expenses

Sales commission to purchase shares	**None**
Commissions to reinvest dividends	**None**
Deferred sales load	**None**
Redemption fees	**None**
Fees to exchange shares	**None**

Annual Fund Operating Expenses
(as percentage of average net assets)

Investment management fees	**0.34%**
12b-1 fees	**None**
Other expenses	**0.91%***
TOTAL EXPENSES	**1.25%***

The total expenses on a $1,000 investment,
assuming a 5% annual return and redemption at
the end of each period:

1 year	3 years	5 years	10 years
$13	**$40**	**$69**	**$151**

DO consider a so-called institutional fund.

The funds we read about all the time—those offered by companies like Fidelity, Janus, and Vanguard—are retail funds designed for individual investors. Even though their minimum initial investments may seem high—$3,000, $5,000, or even $10,000—these antes are quite low compared with those of the funds offered to institutional investors such as pension funds and endowments.

Why then should you consider an institutional fund? For the same reason professional managers, with billions of dollars to invest, use them. They have lower expenses—and often more reliable performance—than retail funds. Until recently, they were available only for single investments of $1 million or more. But now they are trying to get a toehold in the retail market by offering their funds at minimums as low as $1,000 through discount brokers like Charles Schwab & Co. and Jack White & Co. This gives you the opportunity to get in on investments that were formerly available only to investors with millions to put in a single fund.

Ten years ago, institutional mutual funds made a decision to ignore the retail market because it is expensive to maintain small accounts. Further, small investors seemed too fickle, moving their money around too frequently. But that decision has come back to haunt them as the retail marketplace has exploded, approaching $3 trillion in assets.

How to tap into that? They couldn't trade on their names—like Pimco, Pfamco, and DFA—which no retail investor has ever heard of. Advertising wasn't a good option. It's expensive and would boost the fees, canceling out a major advantage of the institutional funds. "Retail is first and foremost a marketing business," says David Booth, chief executive officer of Dimensional Fund Advisors (DFA), an institutional fund group based in Santa Monica, Calif. "The skills you need to be successful are more likely to be developed at Procter & Gamble than at a money management firm. We don't know how to market to retail."

So the institutional funds elected to market through discount brokers like Charles Schwab and Jack White. Here retail investors can buy into the funds with low minimums. And the institutional funds treat the discount broker as a single account. For example, Pimco has pulled in $750 million from the Schwab account within four years. This $750 million is treated like a single account at Pimco, with Schwab as the customer. That means Pimco can maintain its low expenses and avoid marketing and advertising costs.

For the individual investors—probably millions of them—who buy these funds, it means they can share in the top management, proven performance, and low expenses enjoyed by institutions. But there is a catch for individuals, too. The companies that sell these funds—such as Federated, Lazard Frères, and DFA—are not household names. You will not find them on the list of "hot funds" in personal finance magazines. If you want to use institutional funds, chances are you will have to find out about them yourself. You can do that by checking with discount brokers who offer the funds and also by looking them up in Morningstar.

DON'T jump in just before a fund closes to new investors.

34

Closing announcements often pull in huge amounts of **CASH**. Investors who were sitting on the fence or just looking around for a place to put their money believe that they'd better get in under the wire or an important investment opportunity will be lost to them. A fund that is just beyond reach has a certain allure.

In fact, a fund usually closes because it has more money than the manager knows what to do with. That means the opportunity for that fund may have passed, at least for the moment. Awash in money, the fund manager is signaling that he can't find enough good places to put it.

In 1995, reporter Timothy Middleton wrote in *The New York Times* that most funds lagged in performance in the period immediately following the closing. He cited the examples in the chart at right.

Although you shouldn't rush to get into a fund that is about to close, a closed fund that reopens might present a good buying opportunity. Middleton pointed out that when a fund closes, it indicates that the manager is putting investor interests ahead of his own pocketbook. (Because funds make money based on assets under management, the more money in the fund, the more they earn. Consider Fidelity Magellan, the largest mutual fund, with over $50 billion in assets. The management fee, at .76 percent of assets, is a healthy $380 million a year.)

For example, Jean-Marie Eveillard, manager of SoGen International, told Middleton that he closed his fund because the world markets had become so expensive he couldn't put his money to work. The fund's cash level had risen to 30 percent of assets. He said that when prices fell, he would reopen, which he did on March 13, 1995. Similarly PBHG Growth and PBHG Emerging Growth closed in March 1995 because the funds had too much money to invest prudently. PBHG Growth, however, reopened on Jan. 2, 1996.

Excess cash is a particular problem for funds like PBHG, which invest in small companies. But even a fund that buys medium-size companies, like Longleaf Partners, which doubled in assets from New Year's Day to August 1995, can handle only so much money without sacrificing returns. Longleaf took the unusual step of closing both to new shareholders and to existing shareholders on Sept. 15. Typically, a fund will allow existing shareholders to continue to invest.

Here's the best strategy: When a fund announces plans to close, put it on your list to watch for a reopening. Monitor the fund's performance while it is closed by looking up its net asset value in the daily newspaper and compare it with preclosing numbers. Take notes. Watch for news of a reopening in a newsletter like *Morningstar Investor* or *The No-Load Fund Investor*.

RETURNS ON CLOSED FUNDS			
FUND	CLOSED	PRIOR 12 MOS	FOLLOWING 12 MOS
Acorn	July '90	6.5	2.5
SoGen	Feb. '94	29.3	2.1
Windsor	May '89	26.0	2.1

DO consider the vested interest of the seller.

The other day, a friend who works on Wall Street told me about the fabulous weekend she'd just spent. A limo picked her up from work on Friday and whisked her to an elegant spa with a lavish room dominated by a big four-poster bed. She took early-morning hikes through the mountains, followed by yoga and aerobics classes, and enjoyed two daily massages, an herbal facial, body wraps, and marvelous spa food. Expensive? Not for her. She won a contest for selling the most mutual funds from a particular load-fund company.

As it happens, the company was a fine one. And my friend is a fine person. She would never intentionally misguide someone. It didn't occur to her that her clients might not be well served by the funds she sold. Yet hers is one of the more innocent stories. Brokers are subjected to multiple pressures all the time to push certain funds. The incentive might be a vacation in Hawaii. Or it might be keeping their job or getting a promotion. Most large brokerage firms reward brokers based on commissions generated.

Investment houses serve too many masters. If a company is an investment banking client of the brokerage firm, it might be difficult for a research analyst to be candid about the company's stock outlook. If the brokerage is helping to bring a new stock issue to market, it puts

TRAILING COMMISSION *A broker's compensation for keeping investors in a mutual fund, amounting to an annual fee of 25 to 50 basis points, or $1/4$ to $1/2$ of 1 percent of assets.*

pressure on the analyst who is supposed to provide an objective outlook on the stock. The brokers themselves have a number of conflicts, too. When the brokerage brings a stock to market, they may be given a certain portion of that issue to unload. That's part of their job. Brokers also typically get bigger commissions for selling "house products," such as mutual funds marketed by their own firm. And they get bigger **TRAILING COMMISSIONS**, or ongoing commissions, for these products. For example, a broker might get 25 basis points, or $\frac{1}{4}$ of 1 percent of assets, for each year you stay in a mutual fund he sold you. But if he sells you a house fund sponsored by his brokerage, he might get 35 basis points. If he sells $10 million in mutual funds, that's a difference of between $25,000 and $35,000 a year in additional income. Add to that contests and the desire to stay on the right side of the boss.

It's very difficult to determine whether a broker is giving you objective advice. If, say, a Dean Witter broker recommends a Dean Witter fund, is it because it is the best fund for you? Or because he will get a larger annual trailing commission? Perhaps it's just the fund that he knows best.

Whether the motivation is ignorance or greed, you don't want to be stuck with a lemon so that your broker can win a trip to a spa. If you intend to take a recommendation for a fund, ask to see some backup. Why should you buy this fund? Does it meet your objectives? How does it compare with its peers? What was its best year? Its worst year? How does its annual return compare with a benchmark like the S&P 500 index? To know an average annual return is not enough.

DON'T confuse a change in the fund's share price with an investment gain or loss.

Does this describe your investment style? You buy a mutual fund and then look it up in the newspaper each day to see whether its share price, or net assset value, increases. If it doesn't move, you sell it and move on to another one. Equating movements in a fund's **NAV** with investment performance is a common and costly mistake. Consider the Lindner Dividend fund, a solid performer for the past decade. Look at its share price, or NAV, and total return (see graph).

If you looked at the change in the NAV from 1984 to 1995 and used that as the sole measure of performance, you would calculate that the fund gained a measly 12 percent in 12 years. In fact, the fund's total return was 323.98 percent, for an **AVERAGE ANNUAL RETURN** of 12.81 percent over the period.

What's the mystery? Like stocks, mutual funds are introduced at a specific price, or NAV, often $10 for mutual funds. When a stock price moves up from its initial price— or the price you paid for it—it means that your investment is increasing in value. Many investors expect to use the NAV of a mutual fund as the same type of measure. "My own father gives me this problem," says Steven Norwitz, a vice president at T. Rowe Price in Baltimore. "I recommend a fund to him and then he tells me, 'This fund is going nowhere, and I'm going to sell it.'"

The reason a mutual fund cannot be measured like a stock is that the fund manager does a number of things with the portfolio that produce income and capital gains and losses. For example, Lindner Dividend fund is an income fund, which means it pays out a regular dividend. These dividends should be reinvested in the fund. Although the dividend is part of the return and increases your investment, it does not change the share price.

Portfolio managers also buy and sell securities, generating capital gains and losses for the fund. Once a year, the fund manager pays out capital gains, which you can—and should—reinvest in the fund by buying more shares. The capital gains, too, are part of the fund's total return.

When a fund pays out gains, the share price drops to reflect it. This is called "going ex-dividend." If you look at your mutual fund statement, you will see that you received a capital gains distribution that resulted in a purchase of a certain number of new shares. So your investment will be worth the same amount, but you will have more shares valued at a slightly lower NAV.

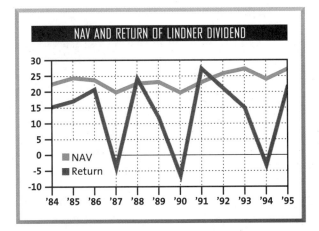

NAV AND RETURN OF LINDNER DIVIDEND

■ NAV
■ Return

DO add to your holdings with an automatic-investment program.

Investing is all about discipline: discipline in buying and discipline in selling. The best way to discipline yourself is with a systematic investment program in which you make regular monthly or quarterly investments no matter what is happening in the market.

Professionals have a name for this "strategy." They call it dollar cost averaging. This is a method of buying mutual fund shares by investing the same amount of money on a regular schedule regardless of the market price. Studies have shown that investors who do this tend to pay less per share over time than those who purchase shares in a block. It works particularly well when buying volatile funds. That's because the same $100 buys more shares when the fund's price is down and less when it's up. When left to our own devices, most of us tend to do just the opposite: we buy a fund when it's "hot" and trade at its high, and we dump it when the price sags.

A number of good fund companies will open an account with no minimum whatsoever, provided you agree to deposit at least $50 a month. Of the 627 fund families in the Morningstar database, 172—or 27 percent—now offer these programs with a minimum initial investment of $100 or less.

To set up a program, call the company and ask for an application. Here are three portfolios to consider, ranging from conservative to very aggressive. (All funds are available for investments of $50 per month. Some require a $100 investment to open the account.)

Conservative USAA Income Stock, an equity

income fund; Spectrum Income; and Spectrum Growth. The Spectrum funds, offered by T. Rowe Price, tap into more than 10 different T. Rowe Price funds, including both domestic and international, growth and income, giving broad diversification.

More Aggressive This portfolio, invested entirely in stocks, needs time to grow. Five years is an absolute minimum; 10 is better. Neuberger & Berman Guardian, a growth-and-income fund, is the cornerstone; Scudder International, one of the oldest and best of the international funds, and Janus Mercury, a relatively new growth fund with a great record, add the zip. (New funds always carry special risk because they don't have track records.)

Truly Aggressive Long-Term This high-risk portfolio invests in emerging markets around the world and in small-company stocks in the U.S. Don't consider it unless you have 10 years and are prepared to ride out the volatility: T. Rowe Price New Asia concentrates on common stocks of companies in the Pacific Rim, excluding Japan. Scudder Latin America taps into another part of the globe that is expected to have explosive growth during the next decade. Both of these funds had spectacular years in 1993 and dismal years in 1994 and 1995. Twentieth Century Ultra is a highly volatile fund offering investment in aggressive growth stocks in the U.S.

Some pros argue that if you have a great deal of money, you should dump it all into the market at once, because you start earning a stock return immediately. Our strategy, though, assumes that you don't have a great deal to invest. Instead, you want to make small, regular investments.

DON'T ignore closed-end funds as an investment.

When investors talk about mutual funds, they usually mean open-end funds. But there are actually two types of investment companies that invest pooled assets of investors. Both buy and sell securities based on the portfolio manager's strategy and outlook.

Here is the difference: An open-end fund sells and buys back shares in the fund each business day. When an investor buys shares, those shares are created; when an investor sells, the shares that are redeemed cease to exist. Thus for an open-end mutual fund, the shares outstanding refer to the number of shares owned by investors.

Both the value of the shares and the number of shares fluctuate from day to day as the value of the securities and the number of investors change. At the end of each day, the securities in the portfolio are valued. That value is divided by the number of investors— or shareholders—in the fund to arrive at a price per share, which is called the net asset value, or NAV. That number is listed in the newspaper the next morning.

The advantages of this open-end structure are numerous and explain the popularity of mutual funds: they are safe, liquid, convenient, and easy to buy and sell.

The closed-end fund is a close cousin. These funds issue a fixed number of shares at an initial public offering. The shares are priced and traded like stocks on major exchanges. The fund company is not responsible for redeeming shares. Here the number of shares outstanding is fixed.

An investor who wants to sell must sell through a broker at the market price. Such a fund's shares do not necessarily trade at its net asset value. They may trade above the NAV, which is called "selling at a premium," or below, called "selling at a discount." The trading price is determined by a variety of things, including supply and demand and the market's perception of the fund's prospects, much like the price of a stock.

Certain types of investments can work better in a closed-end format than in an open-end fund. One good example is one-country funds. Markets in many countries are small and illiquid. The manager of an open-end fund might be forced to liquidate securities to satisfy redemptions in a crisis, such as the devaluation of the Mexican peso in 1994. But the manager of a closed-end fund has complete control over its assets.

Experts like Thomas J. Herzfeld, author of *The Encyclopedia of Closed-End Funds,* say that you should not buy a closed-end fund at the initial public offering. But a savvy investor can often find bargains in funds that are selling at a discount.

For example, Mark Mobius, a well-known emerging markets manager, handles Templeton Developing Markets, an open-end fund with a 5.75 percent load. Investors might be able to purchase a similar portfolio at a discount by buying Mobius's closed-end Templeton Dragon fund. Closed-end funds have lower expense ratios, lower cash ratios, and can sometimes be purchased for 90 cents on the dollar. For more information, look at the publication Morningstar Closed-End Funds or at Herzfeld's encylopedia.

DO read the prospectus.

Investors have the right to receive certain information from the mutual fund company before they invest, as well as the right to receive regular reports on the fund. Most of this stuff makes for dull reading. But it's worth the effort to find out the fund's objectives, restrictions on the portfolio manager, fees, and other charges.

Pay special attention to:

Summary of Expenses Look here for any sales load on purchases or on reinvested dividends, redemption fees, and exchange fees (which means you pay when you trade between funds). Ideally, what you want to see in each of these cases is "none" or "0."

Look also for the annual fund operating expenses, the cost of running the fund. These include the management fee, which covers salaries and administrative expenses, and the 12b-1 fee, which covers marketing expenses. Most funds also have a category called "other expenses," which includes miscellaneous fees.

Avoid funds with 12b-1 fees. This is money that will be subtracted from the fund's assets year after year after year. Be cautious, too, if the fund's total operating expenses exceed 1.3 percent, which is the average for a stock fund. Consider Alger Capital Appreciation. Despite the fact that it was the No. 1 performer of 1995, up 78.6 percent, be wary of its expense ratio of 5.53 percent. Some funds—such as new funds or those that trade abroad—have a good reason to go higher. You want to know what it is.

Look, too, at the example, which the company is required to provide, of what you would pay on a $1,000 investment assuming a 5 percent annual return and redemption at the end of the time period. Here's an example from the prospectus of one good no-load fund:

1 Year	3 Years	5 Years	10 Years
$10	**$32**	**$56**	**$124**

When Sheldon Jacobs, editor of *The No-Load Fund Investor,* surveyed about 100 funds, he found that the projected costs on a $1,000 investment if it were withdrawn after one year ranged from $4 to $93. The 10-year projections ranged from $35 to $306.

Financial History This shows up to 10 years of the fund's performance. Check to see if the fund has cut into net asset value to pay out dividends. Is the expense ratio declining over time or increasing? Is the portfolio turnover rate fairly steady and modest, for example, in the 50 percent range?

Investment Objective This states where the manager will put most of his money. For example, "the fund will invest substantially all of its assets—but no less than 80 percent—in common stocks." How will the rest be invested? What other options does the manager have? Many funds now say, "The fund can invest up to 33 percent in foreign securities." You will also want to know whether the fund can use **DERIVATIVES** and how they can be used.

78

Performance Look at the fund's total return for the past 10 years, which is calculated according to Securities and Exchange Commission regulations. It will be compared with an index, usually the S&P index for a domestic stock fund. Compare the fund to the index, and look for consistency.

DON'T overlook the help available over the phone from no-load companies.

141

Until recently, investors who needed advice on buying mutual funds had little choice but to go to a stockbroker and pay a **LOAD** or commission for the fund. That's no longer the case. As funds that are sold directly over the phone have gained market share, they, too, are beginning to offer advice. "The direct marketing companies have recognized that, with the increasing complexity of financial markets and the hundreds of fund offerings, people need much more assistance in selecting funds and in determining a suitable asset-allocation strategy," says Steven E. Norwitz, a vice president at T. Rowe Price.

This is happening at the same time that advice offered by brokers is coming under increased scrutiny. Brokers face potential conflicts of interest that pit their own compensation against the needs of their clients. For example, they typically receive higher commissions for selling funds that are sponsored by their brokerage firms. Or a firm might offer a sales-incentive program in which a broker can win a free trip by selling a certain investment.

There are a couple of advantages to getting information from no-load companies. The obvious one is that it's free. Second, the advice from a no-load company is arguably more objective than advice from a brokerage firm. The phone sales representative, who earns a salary, has nothing to gain by pushing you into a particular fund. In fact, your conversation is recorded, and the rep knows that if you make a decision you regret based on his advice, he stands to lose. Still, he does want you to pick a fund from his company rather than take your money to a competitor.

As an experiment, I called a dozen good no-load companies to see what kind of information investors could expect. Not once was I pressured to buy a fund or even asked for my name and telephone number. But you should know that not all the advice is as complete as you might need. And you should reject simplistic answers, such as "Our best fund is our international fund." Clearly, the same fund is not right for every caller. A good phone rep will ask you something about your goals and investment experience.

Here are some tips for obtaining information by telephone:

◆ Don't worry about sounding unsophisticated. This is a good place to ask the most basic questions you can think of: What does equity mean? What is a long-term bond? What does a growth and income fund do?

◆ Provide a thumbnail sketch of what you want and ask for recommendations. For example, you might ask which is the company's best middle-of-the-road fund for a core holding. Or you might ask for the most aggressive fund or the best new fund.

◆ Ask which of the company's funds is most highly regarded in the press.

◆ Ask the rep for his or her personal favorite and why.

◆ Don't buy a fund based only on the information you receive from the fund company. But do consider it of value. In many cases, it is more valuable than what you will get from a broker with a vested interest.

DO elect reinvestment of dividends and capital gains.

When you buy a mutual fund, you probably hope that its share price or net asset value will increase over time, because that means your money is growing. But for many funds, it is the reinvestment of earnings that is the real power-house. Mutual fund earnings come from the dividends paid by stocks and the interest paid on bonds and money market funds. Funds also generate **CAPITAL GAINS** and losses when a manager sells securities in the portfolio.

When you open a mutual fund account, you will be asked what you would like to do with these dividends and capital gains. You can either have them reinvested in your account or you can have the money sent to you in a check. For some investors, such as a retiree who is using a portion of investment income for living expenses, electing a payout is O.K. But most people should choose reinvestment.

The ability to reinvest income and capital gains automatically by buying additional shares is one of the clear advantages a mutual fund offers over investing directly in common stock. That's because the bulk of the long-term growth in the stock market, particularly in large-company stocks, comes from this reinvestment rather than from the stock price appreciation.

If you invest in a stock directly, the dividends that stock pays might be paid in cash, which pays no further interest. Or they might be

CAPITAL GAIN *The increase in the price of an asset between its purchase and sale. Capital gains taxes are due on this increase.*

deposited into your money market account at the brokerage, where you earn money market rates on the dividends rather than plowing them back into the stock market. (Many companies offer reinvestment programs, but there is often a fee.)

Consider this: If you had invested $1 in large-cap stocks—those that make up the S&P 500 index—at the beginning of 1926 and reinvested all the dividends, you would have had $1,114.73 at the end of 1995. This is called the total-return index. But if you did not reinvest earnings, your return would be based only on the appreciation in stock prices, and you would have had $48 at the end of 1995. This is called the capital-appreciation index. Small-cap stocks typically do not pay dividends, so the total-return and capital-appreciation indexes are the same. If you had invested $1 in small stocks in 1926, you would have had $2,842.77 in 1995. Small-stock funds do generate capital gains when the portfolio manager trades, and these, too, should be reinvested.

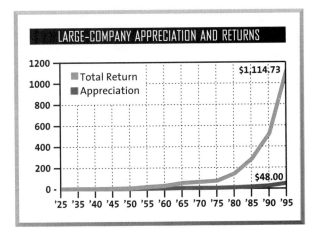

LARGE-COMPANY APPRECIATION AND RETURNS

■ Total Return
■ Appreciation

$1,114.73

$48.00

DON'T buy a market-timing fund for your portfolio.

Countless studies have proved that no one is able to time the market effectively. You should not try to do it yourself. And you certainly shouldn't be paying someone else to do it.

One of the most well-meaning managers of a market-timing fund is Paul Merriman, manager of the Merriman Asset Allocation Fund, based in Seattle. Merriman travels the country meeting with the press and talking at conferences about the advantages of market timing.

Unfortunately, the results of his market-timing decisions have not been entirely positive for his fund. Consider its performance during its first six full years of operation compared with both the S&P 500 Stock Index and the Lehman Brothers Aggregate Bond Index, a measure of the bond market (see graph).

Merriman argues that being out of the market when it falls apart is worth a lot. But the performance of his fund is mediocre at best. On Jan. 1, 1992, even Merriman made something of a concession to the negative image of market timing by changing the name of his fund from Merriman Timed Asset Allocation to Merriman Asset Allocation, although he still moves among domestic stocks, foreign stocks, and domestic and foreign bonds and cash. He often moves to high cash positions—75 percent of the fund was in cash at the beginning of 1995, according to Morningstar.

Market-timing funds have a number of problems. The most obvious one is that it's difficult to time the market. Second is the high expenses incurred in attempting to do so. For example, the Merriman fund had a turnover of 450 percent in 1994. But its expense ratio of just over 1.5 percent is dwarfed by the 2.5 percent of the Rightime fund.

Rightime Blue Chip, a market-timing fund with a longer record, provides a clear example of why it doesn't pay to try to time the market. It outperformed the market three years— 1987, '90, and '94—when the market did poorly. But it underperformed in the years the market did well, often by a big margin. The reason, according to Morningstar analyst Lori Baron, is that manager David J. Rights uses a computer model to decide whether to invest 100 percent in blue chips or to put all the assets in cash. Though the model has been successful in predicting the downturns, it misses the up trends. For example, Rights started 1995 all in cash. The model gave the buy signal in February, but the fund never caught up with peers that started the year fully invested, gaining 29 percent compared with 37 percent for the overall market. "The time may never be right for this offering," Baron concludes.

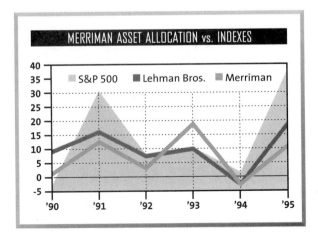

MERRIMAN ASSET ALLOCATION vs. INDEXES

DO read the proxy statement.

A mutual fund is not required to hold an annual meeting each year. However, it must do so if it wants to make changes in investment policy or in the investment advisory contract or sometimes if it needs to elect new directors. In these cases, it must issue a proxy statement announcing the meeting and the agenda. Proxy statements make heavy reading. Take the trouble, though, to look for these things, which you should vote against if you are opposed to them:

Changes in Investment Policy When the Strong Funds sent out proxy statements in spring 1995, the group asked for sweeping changes in the way its funds are permitted to invest. Among them: a fund may purchase real estate–related securities; it may trade commodity future contracts; it may leverage up to one third of the fund's assets (up from 5 percent); it may borrow from or invest in other funds. Strong also asked to make some "fundamental" policies "nonfundamental," so that they could be changed in the future without a vote of shareholders.

Strong argued that it was merely following a trend. In fact, Fidelity Investments and T. Rowe Price had already made such changes, which they called simple bookkeeping. "We had a situation where funds had different investment provisions, not as a matter of intent, but depending on when they were brought out," says Henry Hopkins, chief counsel at T. Rowe Price. "We were trying to standardize our funds."

All of the Strong Funds changes passed. Still, many professional investors decided to drop the Strong Funds because they thought the changes gave its managers too much investment leeway. "One of the biggest problems we have with a portfolio manager is we *don't* know what's underneath his jacket," says H. Lynn Hopewell, an investment adviser in Falls Church, Va. "Everybody's got a reason for asking for more freedom. But who cares?" Be particularly vigilant for requests for changes that will send the fund in a different direction.

Changes in Investment Management Fees Every fund charges shareholders for certain expenses, including fees to pay the portfolio manager. Changes in these fees must be spelled out. In 1995, the Third Avenue Value Fund announced that it would pay manager Martin Whitman 90 basis points, or $9/10$ of one percentage point, up from 50 basis points, or $1/2$ of one percentage point.

Although the fee was not exorbitant, it seemed unfair to shareholders who had invested on the promise of decreasing fees. For example, Don Phillips, president of Morningstar Mutual Funds, had invested when the fund first opened with an expense ratio of 2.5 percent, roughly double the average. New funds typically have high management fees because they have few assets. But Third Avenue said it would decrease the fee as assets grew. At first it did. But Phillips felt the fund broke its commitment to early shareholders with the 1995 increase.

"For four years, I've paid substantially above-average fees," Phillips says. "Now they're renegotiating the contract." Although Phillips won't dump the fund, he'll contribute less money in the future.

DON'T buy gimmicky funds.

There are more than 8,000 mutual funds available today. Are there 8,000 good fund ideas? Hardly. The good funds are the ones that *don't* try to get fancy. They do something you can understand, like buy small-company stocks. The bad ones are usually developed by fund companies during a bear market, when there is little investor enthusiasm for stocks, or during a time of low interest rates, when conservative investors feel they're losing ground with their money in the bank.

Here's an example: Option income funds were developed in 1977, when stock funds were very much out of favor after a long bear market. Mutual fund assets were declining; investors were bored. Sumner Abramson, a portfolio manager at Colonial Management in Boston, hit on a way to give a stock fund a little kick by writing **OPTIONS** to provide extra income.

Abramson didn't buy options, though. He used them conservatively, by putting together an equity portfolio and selling options on all the stocks. If the stocks went up in value, the option holders could call them away. But if they didn't, he could pocket the money from the option sales, adding some income to his stock fund.

Unfortunately, these funds proved to be poor performers in both good markets and bad. After a couple of years, they disappeared.

OPTION *A financial instrument that gives the owner the right to buy (call) or sell (put) the underlying security for a specific price during a specific time period.*

But the gimmicks did not. In 1986, Dreyfus Investments introduced a group of funds that relied on market timing and **DERIVATIVES** to exploit market volatility. The funds shot the lights out in 1987, turning in high double-digit returns as the market crashed. Since then, returns have ranged from mediocre to dismal. Worse yet, heavy trading racks up tax bills that eat up what returns there are.

Add to your gimmicky list the bear-market funds that debuted in 1994, such as Lindner Bulwark, Robertson Stephens Contrarian, and Rydex Ursa. These funds are designed to feed investor fears of a stock decline and to do well when stocks do poorly. But since stocks do well most of the time, these funds will usually lag.

I would also add to the gimmick list market-timing funds, funds that propose to minimize taxes, lifestyle funds, asset allocation funds, and any other type of fund in which the manager proposes to do something other than buy a portfolio of securities that he expects will appreciate.

Your goal is to set up a portfolio that does well in all types of market environments. The best way to do that is by choosing good funds that invest in different classes of assets or that employ different investment styles.

There are a number of legitimate types of funds that can be used to hedge against declines in the stock market. These include real estate funds, natural resources funds, energy funds, and funds that invest in stock markets around the world. But do not buy into a portfolio manager's promise that he can go against the grain of the market and save you from losses.

78

DO invest internationally.

Just one generation ago, U.S. stocks represented two thirds of the value of all the stocks outstanding in the world. Today that statistic has neatly flip-flopped: two thirds of all stock value is to be found outside the U.S. Investing only in this country is far too limiting.

But there are other reasons for investing overseas. Investors should always be looking for different asset classes that perform well in different environments. One of the arguments for investing overseas is that stock markets in different parts of the world tend to hit their peaks and valleys at different times because of varying economic conditions. Although some researchers have found that the negative correlation between foreign and domestic markets has lessened as the world has become a global marketplace, it has not disappeared. For example, Peter L. Bernstein, a financial consultant in New York, says that the two markets that have been most out of step with the United States are Japan and Italy.

Look at the graph of returns of large-cap U.S. stocks compared with foreign stocks, as measured by the Morgan Stanley Europe, Australia, New Zealand, Far East Index (EAFE). There is no clear-cut pattern showing that foreign investments appreciate in value when U.S. investments decline. Still, it is clear from the 12-year totals that investing overseas is worthwhile. "When you put somewhere between 30 to 40 percent of a U.S. portfolio in international

EMERGING MARKETS *The developing countries of the world, where rapid growth is expected as industrialization progresses.*

stocks, you both increase the rate of return and decrease overall **VOLATILITY**," says Mark Holowesko, director of global equity research for the Templeton Funds in Nassau, the Bahamas.

Further, the U.S. economy is mature. Just as some investors look for small U.S. companies that have more growth potential than the blue-chip stocks, others go abroad to countries that are not yet industrialized. Economic growth in the Pacific Rim, Latin America, and other **EMERGING MARKETS** is expected to outpace growth in the U.S. over the next decade.

These emerging markets do not yet move in sync with the U.S. stock market. "The correlation here is zero or negative," says Campbell R. Harvey of the Fuqua School of Business at Duke University. "These markets provide a good hedge against the U.S. market."

Investing in emerging markets requires iron discipline, though. After a dismal 1994, the average fund lost 3.73 percent in '95. But 1996 got off to a good start, with several of the funds up 10 percent in January.

183

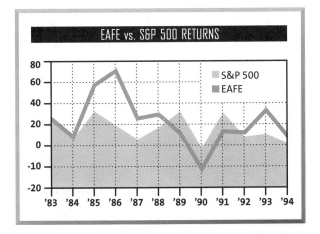

EAFE vs. S&P 500 RETURNS

S&P 500
EAFE

'83 '84 '85 '86 '87 '88 '89 '90 '91 '92 '93 '94

DON'T buy global funds.

Diversifying your portfolio by investing some of your money internationally is an important goal. Buying a global fund is not the best way to do it.

There is a key difference between global funds and international funds. International funds invest exclusively outside the U.S. Some invest only in developed countries; some only in emerging markets. Some exclude particular areas of the world, such as Japan. Some focus on specific areas, such as Europe or the Pacific Rim.

In contrast, global funds are permitted to invest anywhere in the world, including the U.S. A global manager may move money into U.S. markets if he feels that they present the best opportunity. If you have put together your portfolio carefully, you will already have a fund that invests in U.S. stocks. Perhaps you have one for large U.S. stocks and one for small U.S. stocks; one for growth and one for value. You do not want the manager you've chosen for your international fund to duplicate your efforts in this country.

That means that international funds are the best way to invest overseas, because they offer a pure play on foreign stocks. For the same reason, they are more volatile than global funds. If foreign markets do poorly, you can expect international funds to do worse than global funds.

Consider the total returns of international funds, global funds, and the S&P 500 over the past 10 years, as measured by Morningstar (see graph). You can see that in the years that foreign markets did really well—particularly 1986 and 1993—the international funds outperformed the global funds by a wide margin, presumably because the global funds were dragged down by U.S. investments. On the other hand, in the years foreign markets did poorly—like 1990 and 1992—the global funds did better.

In this case, though, you are not looking for the least volatile fund. You should be looking for funds that provide a good deal of diversification and, of course, growth over the long haul.

That said, there is an exception that proves the rule. It is Templeton Growth fund, one of the oldest of the funds that invests around the world, including the U.S. This fund, set up in 1954 by the legendary **VALUE MANAGER** John Templeton, has been managed since 1987 by Mark Holowesko, his protégé. Holowesko follows Templeton's value style of management and includes stocks from emerging markets as well as developed countries. This fund could provide a solid portfolio core.

110

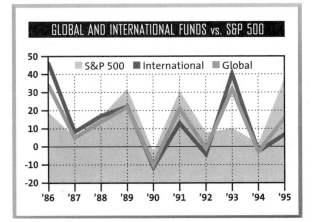

GLOBAL AND INTERNATIONAL FUNDS vs. S&P 500

DO look to see how a fund uses derivatives.

Newspapers and financial magazines were filled with talk of **DERIVATIVES** during the mid-'90s, thanks largely to some spectacularly bad bets on interest rates—and some big losses—by municipalities like Orange County, Calif., and large-company pension funds like Gibson Greetings and Procter & Gamble.

As a result, many advisers warned against using them at all. If big investors can lose a lot of money in derivatives, small investors *don't* belong in them, the reasoning went. Another principle is at work here, too: never invest in anything you don't understand. And who can understand derivatives? Certainly not most individual investors.

T. Rowe Price, a mutual fund company based in Baltimore and known for the high quality of its communications to shareholders, included in a 1995 newsletter a definition of derivatives that is all but impenetrable. When asked about it, Steven E. Norwitz, the T. Rowe vice president responsible for communications, said: "I'm going to be honest with you. I don't understand them myself. That's probably why we didn't have such a good story."

So there is a good argument for avoiding derivatives. But there are two problems with that approach. First, derivatives are part of the

DERIVATIVE *An instrument whose value is "derived" from the movement of a stock, interest rate, market index, or commodity such as wheat, sugar, or coffee. It typically relies on leverage to magnify the effect of price movements in the underlying security or commodity.*

investment scene. Avoiding them is akin to avoiding foods that need refrigeration.

Many common types of investments, such as pools of home mortgages that are sliced up and sold to investors as collateralized mortgage obligations, or CMOs, are technically derivatives, because they are derived from another instrument or security.

The second problem is that most fund prospectuses are written broadly to allow the use of derivatives. Even though the manager may not currently use them, he could change his policy at any time. For example, James A. Engle, comanager of the Winthrop Focus Aggressive Growth fund, a small-company fund, uses no derivatives. But that's just his personal policy. The fund is permitted to use them. And another portfolio manager might see things differently.

A better option is to find out how they are used. Call your fund company and ask when, how, and why a fund uses derivatives. Although the aggressive derivatives get the attention, many derivatives are used to protect against big fluctuations in share price. For example, they might be used by funds that buy securities based in other currencies to hedge against swings in the dollar-exchange rate. This is certainly an acceptable practice.

If you want a more stable foreign-stock fund, you might prefer that it be hedged. But if you want to diversify into other currencies, you don't want the fund to hedge back into the dollar.

The best approach is to become informed about how your mutual fund uses derivatives and how much of the fund's assets are invested in these instruments.

DON'T ignore your mutual fund statements.

Most investors glance at their statements to determine the value of their accounts and then toss them in the trash. But you can use them as an investment and tax-planning tool. "There's been a big change in statements over the past couple of years," says Steven E. Norwitz of T. Rowe Price. "Instead of just providing account value, they include a great deal of information that is helpful in planning."

Bond funds typically send a statement each month to show you the reinvested dividends. Stock funds send a statement when you buy or sell shares, as well as a quarterly or annual statement.

When you get the statement, do look to see the change in the value of your account over the period. You don't want to sell a fund just because the price is down, of course, but you should be monitoring your funds.

If you own more than one fund in the same fund group, or if you own your funds through a discount brokerage, you can look at the overall value of the account and at the asset allocation. Check your current statement against your previous one to see how the allocation has changed.

For example, a T. Rowe Price statement for an investor holding more than one fund breaks down your investments into stocks, bonds, and cash. It shows what percentage of your total portfolio is allocated to each fund. And it shows what percentage is in stocks, in bonds, and in cash. You should not be changing your asset allocation with each statement. But you should **REBALANCE** once a year. Looking at your statement will help you decide how to do that.

If you've sold any shares during the period, take note of the price for tax purposes. Either keep the statement for your records or note the price of the shares in your tax files. Many statements will provide the gain or loss for tax purposes, calculated using the average cost per share.

Some fund statements, such as those provided by Neuberger & Berman, show the current value of your shares as well as your cost basis, which is the amount the shares originally cost, for the purposes of calculating taxes.

That might help you decide which shares to sell. If you wish to sell specific shares, you must notify the company before you make the sale. For example, the statement might say that your shares of XYZ fund are worth $10,000 and that the cost basis is $7,000. Perhaps the shares of ABC fund are also worth $10,000. But their cost basis is $5,000. That means if you sell XYZ, you will owe capital gains tax on $3,000. But if you sell ABC, you will owe tax on $5,000.

The bottom right-hand corner of the Vanguard statement provides a box called Portfolio Allocation, which looks like this:

Portfolio Allocation

Money Market	**10%**
Fixed Income	**10%**
Balanced	**0%**
Equity	**80%**
Total	**100%**

This information can help you see quickly what you need to do to rebalance.

DO read the annual report.

Like a company that makes cars or toothpaste, an investment company that manages money is required to send out a report to shareholders each year with details of its performance. Here are some things you should do with the report:

◆ Compare the fund's annual performance with a performance index. If it is a large-company fund, compare it with the Standard & Poor's 500 Stock Index. If it is a small-company fund, compare it with the Russell 2000. If it is an international fund, compare it with one of the Morgan Stanley international indexes. The benchmark index should be included in the annual report. If not, you can look it up in *Barron's*, the weekly financial newspaper.

◆ Compare your fund with its peer group by looking at the Lipper categories published by Lipper Analytical Services. These figures are also published in *The Wall Street Journal* and *Barron's*. If the fund did poorly, you want to know whether the same was true of the entire group. You should expect your fund to be a consistent performer, ideally in the top quartile of funds in its peer group.

◆ Look at the table that gives year-by-year performance going back 20 years. This is the only place you will get this type of snapshot of the fund's performance history. It helps you determine whether the fund has been a consistent performer or whether its performance is changing over time.

◆ Read the portfolio manager's explanation of the fund's performance and his market outlook. This is particularly important if the fund's performance was different from that of its peer group. Look for a candid appraisal of the market and an explanation of the fund's performance in it. The Vanguard Group has been particularly good in this area, even going so far as to warn investors when a particular industry or market has done extremely well and noting that its bull run might be nearing an end. If the fund did poorly, you want to see what the portfolio manager plans to do about it and when he expects a change.

◆ Check the fund's portfolio holdings. Many of the materials you receive about a mutual fund will provide only its 10 largest holdings. But the annual report lists all the fund's holdings, as well as the percentage allocated to different industry groups. This information is particularly helpful during a period when many mutual funds concentrate in a single industry.

◆ Look at the financial-highlights table, which provides such data as the fund's expense ratio and portfolio turnover rate for the past five years. You want to see whether they are consistent, increasing, or decreasing. The expense ratio should be trending down rather than up. A portfolio turnover rate of 30 to 40 percent is low; 50 to 60 percent might be typical; 100 percent or more is high—that means the manager is turning over the entire portfolio each year. If the turnover rate was 40 percent two years ago and it is now 100 percent, you should find out why.

Don't sell your fund based solely on something you see in the annual report. But do call the fund on its toll-free 800 number and ask for details if you see something that raises a red flag.

DON'T ignore new funds.

Traditional advice to mutual fund investors is this: do your research, buy a fund with a good track record, and then stick with it through thick and thin. For most, it's good advice. But for the more adventuresome, there's an argument to be made for investing in new funds.

Here it is: Many of the top-performing funds specialize in small companies or emerging markets. These two areas have great growth potential. But they require a money manager to be nimble, moving quickly into good stocks. When cash pours into a fund, it can grow too large to be invested efficiently. Some experts also suspect that fund companies pack small funds with their best stock picks, including hard-to-get initial public offerings, to give them an advantage out of the starting gate.

The Value Line Mutual Fund Investor, a mutual fund rating service, conducted a study in 1994 to see if new stock funds did outperform their peers. The study looked at the first-year performance of new funds compared with other funds in the same group. The result: first-year stock funds had a clear advantage over their peers. The opposite was true of bond funds, though.

As the chart shows, the results were most impressive in the small-company category. New small-caps outperformed their peers by nearly 5 percentage points in their first year and continued to outperform—although by only 1 percent—in subsequent years. The performance of new small-company funds was consistent over a 10-year period, the only exception being 1987, when the market crashed.

It will be interesting to watch Garrett Van

Wagoner, who left the Govett Smaller Companies fund at the end of 1995 to set up three Van Wagoner funds. At Govett, which he managed from its inception in December 1992, Van Wagoner racked up a stunning record: up 58.50 in 1993, 28.75 in 1994, and 69 points in 1995, for an average annual return of 51.08 percent. His three new funds are Van Wagoner Micro Cap, which will buy tiny companies; Van Wagoner Emerging Growth, which will invest in small companies; and Van Wagoner Mid Cap, which will buy companies with market capitalizations of up to $4.5 billion. "I believe there is a real incentive to uncover a winner early," says Sheldon Jacobs, editor of *The No-Load Fund Investor* in Irvington-on-Hudson, N.Y. "Once a fund gets big, a few good selections don't mean as much."

That said, new small-company funds carry a great deal of risk. If you are adventuresome, watch for a new fund that is brought out by a proven manager like Van Wagoner.

PERFORMANCE OF NEW FUNDS RELATIVE TO PEERS

FUND TYPE	FIRST YEAR	SUBSEQUENT YEARS
Aggressive Growth	1.38	0.75
Growth	1.63	0.27
Foreign	1.59	−0.60
Income	2.74	0.39
Small Company	4.50	0.76
General Bond	−0.21	−0.13
Government Bond	0.36	0.41
International Bond	1.17	−1.76
Municipal Bond	−0.28	−0.13

Source: Value Line

DO think about how to sell your funds when you need the money.

As you move closer to the time when you need to take your money out of your mutual funds for a major expense, like college tuition or your own retirement, you need a strategy for moving out of the stock market by selling shares of your funds.

There are many options for getting your money. You can have it transferred to your bank or mailed to you, or you may be able to write a check for it. But if you sell the proceeds of a large account all at once, you must pay tax on all your gains. And if you sell when the stock market is off, you will have defeated your purpose of riding out the market ups and downs by investing for the long term.

If you need the money for college, it makes more sense to start moving the money gradually into a **MONEY MARKET FUND** three years before you must begin paying tuition, leaving money for later tuition bills in the stock market for growth.

If you are retiring and you have to begin to use the money you have saved, it makes sense to take out what you need and allow the rest to keep earning income for you. You can do that with a systematic withdrawal plan, offered by most mutual fund families.

With a systematic withdrawal plan, you can redeem a specific dollar amount from your mutual fund account at regular intervals, such as monthly, quarterly, or annually. You can have the check made out to you and use it for living expenses, or you can request that it be paid to a third party, such as your son in college or the bank that holds your mortgage.

Consider this example. Let's say you are ready to retire and you have accumulated retirement savings of $200,000 in a mutual fund that is growing at 9 percent a year. Now you need some of this money to supplement your income. Perhaps you decide you need $20,000 a year. You can ask the mutual fund company to send that to you, paid out in monthly installments, if you like. If your money continues to grow at the same rate, it will last for 26 years.

The Magic Triangle (below) shows how long your money will last, depending on how much it is earning and how much you withdraw each year. The percentage of your principal that you will withdraw is on the left; the earnings are on the right; and the number of years your money will last is where the two intersect. If the intersection of the two lines is off the chart, your money will last forever, provided it keeps earning the same return. For example, if you have $500,000 in an investment that is earning 8 percent and you withdraw $35,000 a year— or 7 percent of your original principal—your money will never run out.

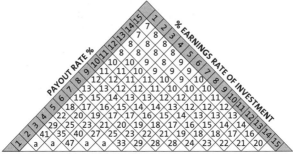

NUMBER OF YEARS MONEY WILL LAST

THE MAGIC TRIANGLE

DON'T be fooled by so-called diversified funds.

One of the benefits of buying mutual funds is that you buy broad diversification across a number of market sectors, right? Sometimes. The Investment Company Act of 1940, which regulates mutual funds, classifies them as either diversified or nondiversified. A diversified fund must spread out 75 percent of its assets by investing no more than 5 percent in any one company. So it must have at least 15 companies in that portion of the fund. The remaining 25 percent may be invested in a single company. So the minimum number of companies a fund could hold to qualify as diversified is 16.

Some funds choose instead to be "nondiversified," allowing them to take a larger stake in a particular stock. For example, in 1995, the Clipper Fund changed its charter from diversified to nondiversified. Janus 20 is another fund that is registered as nondiversified.

But this technicality masks the real issue: many funds that qualify as diversified actually concentrate heavily in whatever market sector is currently hot. The first half of 1995 provided an excellent example. The market exploded in one of the most spectacular rallies in its history, led by the large-company stocks that make up the S&P 500, which was up 20.19 percent for the first six months. I asked Barbara Gertz at Morningstar to compile a list of the diversified stock funds that beat the index, thinking that there might be some lessons to learn from them.

We eliminated sector funds, or those that invest in a particular industry, because some industry segments always do better or worse than the market averages. Gertz found 243 diversified stock funds that beat the S&P 500 index. When we looked at these funds, though, we found that they looked a lot like sector funds. The two hot market sectors in the first half were technology and financial services. Gertz ran the list of winners to see how much each had invested in these sectors. The answer? A lot.

Market weightings can be measured by looking at the S&P index, which has about 10.7 percent in financial services and 9 percent in technology. Most of the funds that beat the index had at least double that weighting in one or the other sector. For example, Alger Capital Appreciation, the No. 1 performer with a return of 45.36, had more than 62.36 in technology. The No. 4 fund, Robertson Stephens Value+Growth, had nearly 80 percent of its assets in technology! And Retirement Planning Growth, another top performer, had triple the market weighting in technology and more than double the weighting in financial services stocks.

Making big **SECTOR BETS** means taking on additional risk. If you owned just three funds and they were all on the winners list, you might feel pretty smug about your investments. But if they were all buying the same stocks, you might have more than half your portfolio invested in technology. So, rather than three diversified stock funds, what you really have is one technology sector fund. Investors in that situation were sadder but wiser when technology funds headed the list of losers in 1995's fourth quarter, as semiconductor stocks took a dive.

206

DO make your 401(k) the core of your mutual fund portfolio.

For many investors, a 401(k) plan *is* their mutual fund portfolio. Without this retirement plan at work, they would have no mutual fund investments. If you are one of them, take great care with your 401(k) plan.

◆ Invest as much as you can. For most Americans, a 401(k) plan represents the single best investment opportunity they have. The money is taken out of your salary before you pay tax on it. If you are in the 30 percent bracket (including state and local taxes), putting $1,000 in a 401(k) saves you $300 in taxes—before your investment has earned a penny.

◆ Most employers match a portion of your 401(k) contribution. For example, your employer might kick in 50 cents for every dollar you contribute up to 6 percent of salary. If you contribute $3,000, you get $1,500 in employer money that would otherwise be lost to you.

◆ Most plans permit loans. That means your money is not out of reach if you need it. You repay the loan with withdrawals from your paycheck. The interest you pay goes into your account.

Once you've decided to make the contribution, how should you invest it? Diversify. If it is your only investment, choose at least three funds. If your plan offers an index fund that follows the S&P 500 Stock Index, that is a good core holding. You might put 40 to 50 percent of your money there.

To diversify, you should have one fund that invests in small-company stocks and one international fund. If you are extremely concerned about variations in your principal, put a portion—perhaps 15 percent—in a fixed-income investment such as a short-term bond fund, a **GUARANTEED INVESTMENT CONTRACT**, or a money market fund.

106

Consider what Don Phillips, president of Morningstar, did with his 401(k) money. Because the company is in the mutual fund business, it took great care in selecting mutual funds for the 401(k) plan, putting together a group of top funds from a number of different mutual fund families.

Some of them were a bit too aggressive for Phillips, who considers himself a conservative investor. For example, he says he would never invest in emerging markets on his own. But he took the plunge with his 401(k) plan, splitting his contributions equally among the 10 funds offered. He reasoned that a retirement account is the best place to make aggressive bets. He keeps his more conservative choices for the rest of his portfolio, which includes money he might need in the shorter term.

If your plan offers aggressive funds, check out their records before investing. Over the past several years, most employers have been revamping their 401(k) plans, thanks to government regulations that suggest offering three diversified options with different levels of risk and potential return. Employers are also upgrading education programs to help employees understand their choices. Take advantage of that and do some research into the funds.

Remember that 401(k) investing allows you to take advantage of **DOLLAR COST AVERAGING**, so it is the best way to invest in more-volatile funds. Also remember to rebalance your 401(k) once a year.

58

DON'T mistake commodity funds for mutual funds.

Commodity futures are traded on a number of exchanges around the country, including the Kansas City Board of Trade, the Chicago Board of Trade, and the New York Mercantile Exchange. Commodities are bulk goods, such as metals, oil, grain, and livestock. The exchanges trade contracts for the future delivery of these goods. For example, a farmer who wants to hedge the price of his fall wheat crop could sell a contract guaranteeing him a certain price. If the market goes down as he begins planting or harvesting, he still gets the contracted price.

The traders on the other side of the deal do not plan to take delivery of a crop of wheat, though. They are speculators who buy and sell commodity futures, hoping that they will earn a profit by guessing which way the price is going. For example, a drought might drive the price of wheat futures up. Excess capacity will drive the price down. Futures prices are very volatile, often moving swiftly and erratically in a single day, simply on rumors of changes in the outlook for that commodity. A speculator will trade in and out of the commodity, unwinding his position before it is time to take delivery. It is important to understand that the trader does not actually have anything of value underlying his trades. He is simply buying and selling a binding agreement to take delivery of the commodity at some future date. If he guesses wrong, he can lose all the money he invests.

Commodity traders also trade for investor accounts, using pools of investor funds to buy and sell commodity and financial futures—

such as those based on Treasury bills or stock market indexes; they, too, are traded on a commodities exchange.

Investors become interested in these funds for two reasons: First, they hear about the sometimes spectacular returns—200 percent, 300 percent, or 400 percent—which dwarf those from investments in any type of stock mutual funds. Second, some studies have indicated that commodities have a negative correlation with stocks and bonds, meaning that when stocks and bonds do poorly, commodities do well. Investors should always be looking for investments that have a negative correlation to their core holdings in stocks.

Most investors don't belong in commodity funds, though. Their risk is too high. With a commodity fund, you could lose everything.

Commodity funds are set up as limited partnerships, not mutual funds. Like the real estate limited partnerships that were popular in the 1980s, they are sold in units. A general partner sets up a fund, collects the money from the limited partners, and assigns a trading manager to trade commodity futures.

Unlike mutual funds, commodity funds are not a short-term, liquid investment. Although the funds do post a **NAV** daily, there is no secondary market for them. You must buy your units from the general partner, and you must sell them back to the general partner.

Many funds impose a stiff exit fee, and they pay the manager a very high fee—perhaps 5 percent or more a year. In addition, the fund is charged with all the trades made, which might rack up expenses of 20 to 25 percent a year. That compares with less than 2 percent on a typical stock fund.

DO think about the impact of taxes on your investments.

There are two ways taxes can bite into your performance. Most investors know that when they sell or trade shares of a fund, they must pay taxes. But many do not know that when the portfolio manager buys and sells securities, the investor must pay taxes on any capital gains generated by the sale.

Mutual funds do not pay taxes on their earnings. The earnings are passed on to you and the other shareholders, and you are responsible for paying taxes as if you owned the securities yourself. These earnings might be paid out to you as income, or they might be reinvested in your account. Either way, you owe the taxes.

At the end of each year, your mutual fund company will send you IRS Form 1099-DIV, reporting your income for the year. The fund company also reports it to the IRS. And you must, too. Even if you have invested in a tax-free fund, you will receive a form and you must report the tax-free income on your tax return.

There is something you can do to reduce taxes on the shares you trade. It requires careful record keeping. If you sell shares at a loss during the year, you can use the capital loss to offset any taxable capital gain. If losses exceed gains, you are allowed to deduct the excess loss from your regular income, up to $3,000. To track your capital gains and losses, you need records of when you made your investments,

COST BASIS *The price of an asset that is used to calculate capital gains tax.*

how much you invested, the price you paid for each share, and how many shares you bought. Reinvested dividends are the same as purchases for record-keeping purposes.

Good records allow you to reduce your taxes in another way. You can instruct the mutual fund company to sell the shares you paid the most for first, reducing your capital gain, and so your current tax bite. Perhaps you bought 100 shares of a fund at $10 a share some years ago. Last year, you bought another 100 shares at $20 per. Now the fund is selling at $25, and you need to raise some money. You want to sell 100 shares, which will net you $2,500 at today's price. If the fund company redeems the 100 shares that you bought at $10 a share, your **COST BASIS** is $1,000 and your capital gains $1,500. But if you ask the fund company to redeem the 100 shares that you bought at $20 a share, your cost basis is $2,000, and your capital gain for tax purposes will be only $500.

Some companies require their managers to use this method—called the specific identification method—when they sell securities in order to reduce taxes for shareholders.

To sell the highest-priced shares first, you must write to the mutual fund company in advance and identify the shares you want to sell. For example, you might write: "On April 1, 1996, I plan to sell the 100 shares of XYZ fund that I purchased on March 1, 1995, for $20 per share."

In order to use the long-term capital gains rate, which is currently 28 percent, as opposed to the short-term capital gains, which is the same as ordinary income, you must have held the shares you sell for at least one year.

DON'T neglect an annual performance review.

This is the time that you determine how your funds have performed and rebalance your portfolio so that you maintain the **ASSET ALLOCATIONS** you have set up.

Collect all your statements, including those from the end of the previous year. If all your funds are in the same family, or if you bought them all through a discount brokerage such as Charles Schwab, Jack White, or Fidelity Investments, you will have a single statement. That will make things easier. Some fund groups even show you what percentage of your account is in each fund and what portion is in stocks, bonds, and cash.

If your statement does not do that, organize your funds into those three categories. Then look at your actual asset allocation to see how it has diverged from your target strategy. Even if you made no investments during the year, your allocation has probably been altered by movements in the markets.

If it has, you must rebalance, which simply means selling off the portion that has performed well and buying more of the asset class that did poorly. This is perhaps the most difficult thing for most investors to do, because it is counterintuitive.

But if you have selected your funds carefully and they are each doing the job they were chosen to do, you will be putting money into those that have underperformed because they were out of favor in the market. This is the disciplined way to "buy low and sell high."

This is also the time when you should make certain that each fund is doing what it is supposed to do. Do that by calculating the overall performance of your portfolio and comparing it with market indexes.

The report will provide the value of each fund. But calculating the change might require some work on your part. Look at the value of accounts at the beginning and end of the year and determine the difference.

If you did not buy or sell shares during the year, the calculation should be fairly simple. If you took money out of the account during the year, you might just subtract that amount from the beginning value. Although it will not be accurate to the penny, it will give you a rough idea of the change in value.

Calculate the performance of your stock, bond, and cash portions. If the value of your stock account is up 10 percent and the market is up 15 percent, you want to know why.

This is a way to spotlight funds that are not keeping up. If you selected extremely aggressive funds, you might have one or two that pulled your account down. Examine those funds and make certain that their performance is still within limits you feel comfortable with.

Look at the fund's annual report to read what the portfolio manager says about performance and expectations. Was this one bad year for the fund, or the second or third year in a row that it lagged?

Does the fund have a new manager? Has the strategy shifted? Research the fund in Morningstar Mutual Funds to find the objective comments of an analyst. You should not plan to sell a mutual fund just because of one year's underperformance. But you should keep an eye on it.

DO consider real estate funds.

108

Real estate can be an important asset class to balance a portfolio, because it tends to have a negative **CORRELATION** with stocks. In other words, when stocks do poorly, as in times of inflation, real estate does well. However, most pros have been unhappy with the vehicles available to invest in it. For example, the real estate limited partnerships sold so actively in the mid-'80s burned a lot of investors when Congress changed the tax rules.

Real Estate Investment Trusts, or REITs (pronounced "reets"), are companies that are traded on stock exchanges and that manage portfolios of real estate. Some, called equity REITs, buy real estate and pass on income and capital gains to shareholders. Others, called mortgage REITs, lend money to developers and pass on interest income to shareholders. Some REITs mix the two.

Until recently, the mutual fund industry has not had much to offer in the way of real estate funds. The Fidelity Real Estate Investment Portfolio, set up in 1985, is the oldest and largest fund. But recently companies such as CGM, Crabbe Huson, and Selected/Venture Advisers have offered new funds.

These funds have a low correlation with stocks, as measured by something called **R-SQUARED**. The average real estate fund has

---

R-SQUARED *The percent of movement in a particular security that is explained by the movement in an index. A stock that moves in tandem with the S&P 500 would have an R-squared of 100, because 100 percent of its movement is explained by the movement of the S&P.*

an R-squared of 13.8 to the S&P 500 and an R-squared of 8.6 against the Lehman Brothers Aggregate index. "These are really tiny numbers and show a strong negative correlation," says Jim Raker, a Morningstar analyst. And real estate funds are not particularly volatile. One of the things that prevents volatility is their income. REITs are required to pay out 95 percent of their net income to shareholders.

Although real estate funds are one logical choice for a portion of your portfolio that provides an inflation hedge, picking a fund from the dozen or so offerings has not been an easy task. In 1995, Morningstar took note of the funds as a subset important enough to deserve its own category. That will make picking one from the group easier.

Financial planners are beginning to use real estate funds as an asset class, too, thanks in part to studies that show that real estate does have an inverse correlation to stocks. Their favorites are Cohen & Steers Realty and PRA Realty, both of which are pure REITs, rather than funds that mix REITs with construction stocks and other securities that would do well when the real estate market booms.

Although some investors buy the REITs themselves, financial planners typically use the mutual funds. For example, Deena Katz, a financial planner in Coral Gables, Fla., says, "I buy real estate mutual funds instead of REITs for the same reason I buy stock mutual funds instead of stocks: I want a diversified portfolio."

Note: Not everyone agrees that REITs are a separate asset class. Barry Vinocur, editor of the *Realty Stock Review*, views them as a sector, like technology or health care. But he still considers them a good investment.

DON'T stick with a bond fund that is maintaining its payout by returning your principal.

Time was that investing in bonds was straight-forward. You invested your principal—say $1,000—at a set interest rate of perhaps 5 percent and collected $50 a year in interest income. The value of the bond might change between the time you purchased it and maturity. But that didn't matter to you unless you wanted to sell it. If you held on until maturity, you got your $1,000 back.

199

BOND FUNDS have changed all that. When interest rates rise, the value of bonds in the fund declines. Bond fund managers may not hold the bonds until maturity, so they may not get the full principal back. These complications can plague the best of funds.

But some bond funds virtually guarantee that you won't get your whole principal back at bond maturity because they juice up the income payments by returning a portion of your principal. Here's how that works. Suppose you are a retiree who invests $100,000 in a bond fund that is paying out 7 percent. You need this money to live on, so you elect to take the income in quarterly checks, receiving about $1,750 each quarter.

Suppose bond market conditions change and the fund generates less income. The fund should pay you less, right? That's what the best of them do. But many funds—including some of the largest ones—continue to pay the same $1,750, bolstering the decreased income with a portion of your principal.

The problem for you, the retiree, is that you are spending what you believe to be income.

Only when you cash in your bond fund do you discover that you have spent some of your principal. To determine how common the practice is, Morningstar Mutual Fund publisher John Rekenthaler studied bond funds over two periods. One started Nov. 1, 1986 and the other Oct. 1, 1991; both ended Sept. 30, 1994.

The periods were selected because interest rates were similar at their beginnings and ends, and so they represented what Rekenthaler called a "neutral" environment. In theory, a fund's net asset value should also be about the same at their beginnings and ends. In practice, investors who spent their distributions during those periods lost about 1 percent a year. Many lost more than twice that.

Unfortunately, it is very difficult to determine which funds are paying out principal. "It is simply not possible to understand a fund's accounting practices from its publicly available documents," Rekenthaler says.

He did identify nine bond funds that did a good job of preserving principal: Federated Intermediate, Benham Treasury Note, Vanguard F/I Long Treasury, Columbia Fixed-Income, Scudder Income, Vanguard F/I Long Corporate, Strong Government Securities, Princor Government Securities, and Fidelity Mortgage Securities.

Rekenthaler suggests that investors who wish to use bond funds stick with funds that have low expenses. Expenses are particularly critical for bond funds. A fund with high expenses is more likely to turn to accounting tricks to boost payout. "Those who purchase a fund with an expense ratio of less than 0.5 percent can rest fairly secure that the fund will pay out just what it earns," Rekenthaler says.

DO consider a "fund of funds" for a specific purpose like a college account.

A fund of funds is one mutual fund that invests in a number of other funds, providing an entire portfolio in a single fund, sometimes for an investment as low as $500. Too bad, then, that most of them are not worth considering.

During the 1920s, the fund-of-funds concept was used to create confusing layers of funds that allowed the managers to take the money while the investors weren't looking. Likewise, Bernard Cornfield set up the Fund of Funds in the 1960s, which made millions for the managers at the expense of the investors. Because multifund investing has such a check-ered past, the SEC looks very carefully at new proposals for such funds. That means the ones introduced are carefully scrutinized, but it does not necessarily mean they are a good investment. Three good all-purpose choices do what they set out to do: Vanguard STAR, Spectrum Growth, and Spectrum Income.

The advantage of these funds is instant diversification. You probably know by now that one fund does not provide adequate diversifi-cation. A fund of funds spreads your money across 6 to 10 funds.

The disadvantage is high fees. In most cases, you pay two layers of management fees. First you pay the fees for the funds themselves, then you pay another manager to assemble the group of funds. Consider the Rightime Fund, set up in 1985 to invest in other mutual funds. The fund initially had expenses of 3.19 per-cent, more than twice that of the average stock fund. Although the expenses have trended down over time, they are still in the 2.5 percent range. Worse yet, the fund's performance rarely beats the S&P 500 index. You would be better off in a low-cost S&P index fund.

Similarly, in 1995, Robert Markman, a Minneapolis money manager, set up three Multi-Fund Trust funds, each with a different objective: conservative growth, moderate growth, and aggressive growth. Markman said he would cap his own management fee at 95 basis points. But that still cuts nearly 1 percentage point off the returns you could get by investing in the funds directly.

The bottom line is, if you plan to build a portfolio of funds yourself, you do not need a fund of funds. If you can't bear to pick funds or if you have a single purpose, such as a college account that you don't want to spend time with, you might be well served by these:

◆ Vanguard STAR fund, which is made up of nine Vanguard stock, bond, and money market funds, is a very steady performer with low volatility. Equally important, Vanguard does not add a second layer of expenses. You pay only the underlying expenses of the funds.

◆ T. Rowe Price took the concept one step further with Spectrum Growth and Spectrum Income. Growth invests in six stock funds, including an international. Income invests in seven income funds, which are spiced up by an international bond fund and an equity income fund. These funds do not add a second layer of fees. Their advantage over STAR is the inclusion of foreign funds and the opportunity to pick either growth or income—or to put both together. The income fund is also a good choice for a mostly stock portfolio that needs a little income exposure.

DON'T stick with a fund if the manager doesn't.

You should always be on the lookout for change at a fund that you own or one that you are considering. If the portfolio manager leaves, you leave, too—with him, if you can. A fund's track record belongs to the portfolio manager, not to the fund. There is no reason whatsoever to stick with a new manager. One notable exception is a fund that has a true committee approach, with no one lead manager. Dodge & Cox is one good example of that strategy.

At most funds, the **PORTFOLIO MANAGER** is the star. The brightest star in fund history was Peter Lynch, who left the Fidelity Magellan fund in the middle of 1990. His successor, Morris Smith, spent only two years on the job and was replaced by Jeffrey Vinik in the middle of 1992. Although Vinik may well continue to perform, who knows? The only reason I see to stick with Magellan is that it represents a brand name, like KitchenAid or Whirlpool. Some investors must worry: what if I sell and the fund continues to outperform? Forget about that. The fund is not the same fund that Peter Lynch managed in the 1980s. You can do better elsewhere.

Even if the fund company replaces the departing manager with a big name, tread carefully. For example, when Elizabeth Bramwell left Gabelli Growth in 1994, Mario Gabelli took over the fund himself. Not to worry with a manager like Gabelli, right? Actually, Gabelli is a value manager, and the fund Bramwell managed was set up as a growth fund, so it was a poor fit. In 1995, after mediocre results, Gabelli found a new manager for the growth fund.

Sometimes change creates opportunities. When Donald Yacktman left Selected American Shares to set up the Yacktman Fund in 1992, loyal fans moved along with him, eager to get in on the ground floor with a tested manager. In this case, there was reason to take a second look at Selected American Shares too. After two different interim managers in a short time, the management company assigned Shelby Davis, a portfolio manager who had built a stellar record at New York Venture, to the fund. New York Venture has a 4.75 percent sales charge; Selected American Shares is a no-load. That allowed careful observers their first opportunity to get Davis's management without paying a load.

Investment pros follow the careers of top managers to see when they might get such an opportunity. For example, Don Phillips, Morningstar's president, watched Martin Whitman develop a unique value or "vulture" investment style, picking at securities that no one else would touch. When Whitman opened Third Avenue Value Fund in 1990, Phillips jumped at the opportunity to invest with him. By the end of that year, Whitman added a sales charge to the fund. Then in 1995, he removed the load again, creating another window of opportunity.

Similarly, Garrett Van Wagoner, a star small-company growth picker, left Govett, a load group, to set up his own no-load funds at the beginning of 1996. The best way to keep abreast of these opportunities is to subscribe to a newsletter like *Morningstar Investor* or *The No-Load Fund Investor*.

DO rebalance.

Once you've considered your goals and carefully put together a portfolio, including different types of funds, is your work is finished? Not quite. Even if you are a buy-and-hold investor (and you should be), your portfolio has to be tended. Think of it as weeding a garden. You've selected the plants well, now you must control their growth. For many investors, this is the toughest part.

If you pick a winner and it takes off, chances are you feel proud of your investment prowess. Why prune it back? Because it's not giving the other investments a space in the sun. When you put together your portfolio, you selected different types of funds that would do well in different market climates. Left untended, your portfolio will grow toward the market sector with the best recent performance.

Consider this simplistic example. Suppose you have 50 percent in an S&P index fund, 25 percent in a small-cap fund, and 25 percent in an international fund. If international funds doubled last year while U.S. stocks had a pretty miserable year, perhaps you now have 50 percent in international funds, 20 percent in the S&P index, and 30 percent in small-company funds (because they did better than the larger funds in our example).

It's tempting to stick with your winners. But it is this emotional attachment to investments that trips up most investors. If you understand

GUARANTEED INVESTMENT CONTRACT *A contract between an insurance company and an investor that pays a set rate of interest and guarantees the return of principal.*

market cycles, you know that what goes up comes down. International funds, too, will have their down cycles.

Rebalancing—if it is done rigorously and unemotionally—helps you to do what all investors want to do: buy low and sell high. It encourages making contrarian plays because you are selling the investments that have done well and buying those that have done poorly. In our example, the U.S. stocks will have their run-ups, too. If you rebalance, you will catch them before they start to move.

Consider what Brian Ternoey, a principal at Foster Higgins, benefits consultants in Princeton, N.J., did with his 401(k) portfolio when his employer offered only two options: a stock fund and a **GUARANTEED INVESTMENT CONTRACT**, or GIC. Ternoey, whose specialty is 401(k) management, knows that stocks have the best return over time. So he knows that a retirement portfolio should be chiefly in stocks. But he also knows that diversification is important. Ternoey put 75 percent in the stock fund and 25 percent in the GIC. Once a year, he rebalances his portfolio. If stocks have had a good year and have grown to 85 percent, he sells off a bit, bringing the stock portion back to 75 percent. If they've had a bad year, he adds to the stock fund to bring his portfolio into line.

The key to rebalancing is to remove all emotion from it. Don't try to guess when it's time to sell one fund and buy another or to redirect your investments. That amounts to trying to time the market, which cannot be done successfully. Instead, pick a date, perhaps the first day of the year, and ruthlessly sell off the winners and add to the losers.

DON'T own more than a dozen funds.

If three funds is something of a minimum in order to achieve a diversified portfolio, then 12 funds is something of a maximum. Even an investor with significant assets can put together a diversified portfolio with a dozen funds.

Owning more causes problems in a couple of ways. First, experts say that most investors who own dozens of funds have not thought through a strategy. They simply add new funds as they see an advertisement or read a newspaper or magazine article about a fund. Some investors choose a new fund each year for their retirement money, disregarding what they already have and how the new fund fits in.

The second problem with holding scores of funds is that many of the investments will overlap. That means you will not achieve real diversification. And you will pay more, because you will be paying expenses on each of the funds.

To be well diversified, you want a group of funds that will perform differently in any given type of market. Investors refer to the way funds perform relative to one another as their **CORRELATION**.

If two funds correlate 100 percent, they always move in lockstep. That is expressed as a correlation coefficient of 1, or perfect positive correlation. For example, the Vanguard Index 500 always moves in lockstep with the Standard & Poor's 500 Stock Index, although the

CORRELATION   *The relationship between two different properties. Investors look for investments that have a negative correlation—those that do well in different market environments.*

Index 500 has a slightly lower return, because of expenses.

Perfect negative correlation is expressed as a correlation coefficient of –1. Of course, few pairs of investments move either in lockstep or in totally opposite directions. Most are somewhere in between. But the closer their correlation coefficient is to 1, the more they move together. Investment professionals consider investments with a correlation coefficient higher than a .75 to have a high positive correlation.

Many investors buy a group of well-known funds believing they have achieved good diversification. But large funds are likely to hold the same well-known stocks that are touted by research reports.

A correlation coefficient measures the movement relative to one another of two investments, not of an entire group. Consider the correlation of several other large funds to the Janus Fund for the period of March 1990 to March 1995:

Fidelity Asset Manager	**.79**
Fidelity Contrafund	**.96**
Fidelity Growth & Income	**.95**
Fidelity Magellan	**.89**
Fidelity Puritan	**.70**
Twentieth Century Ultra	**.89**
Vanguard Index 500	**.95**
Vanguard/Wellington	**.92**
Vanguard/Windsor	**.75**

Clearly, in terms of diversification, none of these funds would make a particularly good match with Janus. Nor would owning all nine of them give you much more diversification than owning Janus alone.

DO use a mix of investment styles.

As you diversify your portfolio, make sure you include both large-company and small-company stock funds and that both growth and value stock-picking styles are well represented. These different styles perform well in different environments. Here is a thumbnail description of the styles:

Value Investing A value stock picker attempts a rough valuation of companies by taking apart their balance sheets, looking at their various businesses, and estimating their break-up value. Then he buys those that look cheap.

Two of the best-known value investors are John Neff, who retired at the end of 1995 from managing the Vanguard/Windsor fund, and Michael Price, who manages the Mutual Series funds. Price doesn't hesitate to buy companies in bankruptcy. He took a big position in R.H. Macy & Co., the New York–based department store, in 1990, when it went into bankruptcy. When the company turned around, Price was well rewarded.

Value investors, like Price, never buy on instinct, only on the numbers. "This puts a floor under the company," Price says. "If you buy a company that is seriously undervalued, you really can't get hurt too badly."

Value investors also typically have a formula for selling a stock. When a stock reaches some predetermined measure of value, they dump it.

Growth Investing Growth managers look for companies that are growing much faster than the rest of the economy, never mind how much they cost. They are willing to pay a higher price for a rapidly growing company because they believe the stock price will appreciate much more rapidly, too.

Mark Seferovich, manager of United New Concepts, sticks with small-company growth stocks because he thinks that's where he can get the biggest appreciation. "The revenue growth rates should be 25 percent or more if I find the right companies," Seferovich says. "The sin of paying too much can be overcome if you're in the right part of the growth curve and you can ride it to the top."

Growth managers don't care if a company is cheap. They believe that it's cheap for a reason and may well stay that way.

As you build your portfolio and diversify, you should include at least two growth funds—one that invests in small companies and one that invests in large companies—and two value funds. Here are some top funds to consider:

Small- to Mid-Cap Growth
- Brandywine Fund
- PBHG Growth
- Wasatch Aggressive Equity

Large-Cap Growth
- Harbor Capital Appreciation
- Vanguard Index 500 Trust

Small-Cap Value
- Fidelity Low-Priced Stock
- T. Rowe Price Small-Cap Value
- Royce Micro-Cap
- Mutual Discovery

Large-Cap Value
- Dodge & Cox Stock
- Longleaf Partners
- Vanguard/Windsor II
- Clipper Fund

DON'T buy a load fund without determining that there's something special to justify it.

Numerous studies show that there is no difference in total return between load funds (those that charge a commission) and no-load funds (those that are sold direct over the phone or by mail without a commission) when they are adjusted to reflect the load. The load is not used to hire a better manager; it goes to pay a commission to the salesperson. The most obvious reason to consider a **LOAD FUND**, then, would be to get advice on which funds to buy. Investment professionals consider the funds offered by American Funds in Los Angeles and Putnam Investments in Boston to be the finest load offerings for this purpose.

When you buy a load fund, the commission is subtracted from your payment *before* it is invested. If you invest $1,000 in a fund with an 8.5 percent load, $85 is subtracted as a sales charge, and only $915 is invested for you.

Not long ago, 75 percent of the funds sold were load funds. As investors have become more sophisticated and refused to pay commissions on mutual funds, that proportion is shifting closer to 50-50. That means there are many good funds available without loads, and most experienced investors prefer to do their own research and buy those funds.

There are still some instances, though, when you might consider a load fund. For example, Fidelity Investments, which sells its funds directly over the phone and by mail, has nonetheless added loads of 2 percent and 3 percent on many of them. These loads go to the fund company rather than to a salesperson. Many confirmed no-load investors pony up for these funds, even though they may resent it, because Fidelity offers specialized funds that they cannot find elsewhere. Good examples are the **SECTOR FUNDS** that invest in particular industries. These funds, which carry a 3 percent load, are often the hottest performers in the market and the only way to make a bet on semiconductors, electronics, or the entertainment industry, for example.

206

Other investors are willing to pay a load for an outstanding portfolio manager. For example, many mutual fund managers paid 5 percent to buy Colonial Newport Tiger because they believe manager John Mussey is the finest stock picker available for the Pacific Rim. It is the only mutual fund that Joe Mansueto, founder of Morningstar Mutual Funds, chooses to invest in. All of his other investments are individual stocks. Even though T. Rowe Price offers a no-load New Asia fund, many professional investors don't think it has the depth of management of Newport Tiger.

Even Don Phillips, Morningstar's president and a confirmed no-load investor, decided to pay the 6.5 load to buy FPA Paramount and put some money under the management of William Sams. But when he called the company, he was told that he would have to put the order through a broker rather than buying direct. So he changed his mind.

The bottom line is to look carefully at alternatives before paying a commission for a fund, particularly if you are doing the research yourself. Consider a load fund only to get the talents of a unique manager or to get a toehold in an industry or part of the world that is not represented in the no-load market.

DO consider getting help from a fee-only financial planner.

Not long ago, a friend who writes about mutual funds, personal finance, and financial planning sold a business that he had built up. He received about $1 million—much more money than he'd ever had before. He probably knows every mutual fund available and has written about and recommended any number of them to readers. But when it came to investing the money that represented college for his son and retirement for himself and his wife, he just couldn't decide how to do it. He decided to get help.

You, too, might decide to get professional advice. Be very careful in selecting your adviser. You do not want a stockbroker or anyone with a vested interest in selling you a certain product. Nor do you want someone with a CLU (chartered life underwriter) or ChFC (chartered financial consultant) designation. These people are trained by the American College in Bryn Mawr, Pa., to sell insurance. If you ask someone who sells insurance for help with investments, chances are you will end up with an insurance product such as a variable annuity.

Financial planning is still an unregulated profession, which means anyone can assume the title of financial planner. That puts the responsibility on the client to sort through education, credentials, and know-how.

Planners use a lot of letters behind their names. Some of them are meaningless. It's hard to tell what the others mean. For example, many planners are lawyers and use JD or LLD. It's fine to have a law degree. But that doesn't show any particular competence in investing. Similarly, a CPA may be very knowledgeable. But you don't know that he has expertise in personal finance unless he has also earned the "personal financial specialist" designation, or PFS, from the American Institute of Certified Public Accountants. This is a meaningful designation. (Call 800-TO-AICPA and ask for CPAs who have earned it.)

The designation that is emerging as the most meaningful one in the field is CFP, or certified financial planner. Planners must meet the education, examination, experience, and ethics requirements established by the International Board of Standards and Practices for Certified Financial Planners in Denver.

This group has recently revised its exam and upgraded standards for eligibility. Call the Institute of Certified Financial Planners (800-282-PLAN) for CFPs in your area. If a planner does not have either the PFS or CFP designation, you should wonder why. Anyone can join the International Association for Financial Planning (IAFP) in Atlanta. But there are stiff requirements for getting into the IAFP's Registry of Financial Planners. (Call 800-945-IAFP and ask for a registry member in your area.)

Interview three candidates. Ask if there is a charge for the interview. Questions to ask:

◆ How do you charge for services?
◆ Can you give me names of three professionals (lawyers, accountants, tax specialists) you work with?
◆ How long have you been doing planning in this community?
◆ Are you a registered investment adviser?
◆ Has a client ever filed a complaint against you?

DON'T use gold funds.

203

Not every type of investment is suitable for use in a mutual fund. The idea behind **GOLD FUNDS** is to offer an inflation hedge—something that does well when stocks and bonds do poorly. Unfortunately, it doesn't work.

Here's the story behind gold: Gold has its own fan club, a group of fervent believers, dubbed "goldbugs," who think it is the only true source of value and the time is always right to own it. Reality is a bit different. The price of gold was fixed at $35 an ounce in the U.S. from 1934 to 1971, and individuals were prohibited from owning it. When the fixed price was lifted, the price tripled in two years. In 1974, the ban against private ownership was lifted, and speculation drove the price up still higher, to about $200 an ounce. Then the price fell back to the $170 range until the roaring inflation of the 1970s, when the price of gold skyrocketed, hitting $875 an ounce on Jan. 21, 1980. But when inflation cooled, gold dropped back to the $300-to-$500 range.

As this history shows, the price of gold is volatile and unpredictable. Gold is not a growth investment, like stocks or real estate, which increases gradually, albeit unpredictably, over time. In fact, there is an old saw that throughout history an ounce of gold would buy a decent man's suit. During Roman times, it bought a toga. And today, it will buy a decent department-store suit. That doesn't argue much for it as a long-term investment. (Some aggressive strategies for trading in and out of gold can be found on page 204.)

Not so long ago, it was thought that gold protected a portfolio against inflation. But there is no longer evidence that gold acts as an inflation hedge, either. A good test of an inflation hedge is whether a commodity increases in value when bonds decrease in value. That's because bonds do poorly during times of inflation or fears of inflation. During the 1990s, gold did not perform well during bond bear markets.

So the value of gold as an investment is questionable. But investing in gold mutual funds presents yet another problem. Gold funds do not offer a "pure play" on gold. Most gold funds are "managed" to move in and out of gold-mining stocks and other precious metals as the manager sees fit.

Even if you do like the outlook for gold, investing in a gold fund is no guarantee that you will be investing in it. Consider this: In 1982, the price of gold dropped more than 15 percent. But the average gold fund was up nearly 50 percent. What this means is that gold-fund managers attempted to move their assets out of gold to more attractive investments. That's not what you want as an investor. You want a pure play on a particular asset class. That is difficult to find with gold.

Gold and precious-metals funds used as an asset class to hedge against inflation are losers. So, too, are their records as a long-term investment. Consider the 10-year annualized returns of the top metals funds ranked by Morningstar through early 1995. They were erratic, and most were dismal. True, the top performer, Oppenheimer Gold, had an average annual return of 11.25 for the period. But the 10th best, Invesco Strategic Gold, returned an average of .14 percent a year for 10 years.

DO consider natural resources funds as an inflation hedge.

You should not be moving into the stock market when you think it will go up and out of it in anticipation of a downdraft. But you might consider putting a small portion of your portfolio into an asset class that does well when stocks do poorly. Although there is no perfect **HEDGE** against inflation, it's still worth looking for something to help insulate your portfolio. Natural resources funds are one possibility.

John Rekenthaler, publisher of Morningstar, makes the argument for natural resources funds, which invest in stocks of companies that own or develop natural resources, such as paper, metals, or energy companies, or companies that supply natural resources companies, such as energy service companies.

To prove his point—that this group acts as an inflation hedge—Rekenthaler looked at seven quarters when the bond market had a negative total return. Inflation—or fears of inflation—drives the bond market down. So Rekenthaler wanted to see how gold and natural resources funds performed during the periods when bonds did poorly. His reasoning was this: a fund that does well when bonds do poorly works as an inflation hedge.

Rekenthaler used the Vanguard Bond Index fund, which follows the Lehman Brothers Aggregate Bond Index, as a proxy for the bond

HEDGE *A transaction that offsets—or blunts—another transaction. A farmer might hedge the risk of falling wheat prices by selling wheat futures contracts.*

market. The Bond Index fund began in 1987.

Rekenthaler identified seven quarters when the bond fund had a negative return. Then he looked at the performance of the Vanguard Gold fund, which he considers to be a very good gold fund, during these periods. He also looked at T. Rowe Price New Era, set up in 1969 and the granddaddy of the natural resources funds. New Era is a diversified resources fund; it includes some gold. He also looked at Fidelity Industrial Materials, which invests in chemicals, metals, building materials, but no gold whatsoever, because he considered it more of a pure play on resources.

As Rekenthaler notes, there is no perfect hedge against inflation. But the natural resources funds are a much better option than gold, which performs erratically and had a positive return in only two of the seven quarters when bonds were down. New Era did much better, with a gain in four of the seven quarters. But Fidelity Select Industrial Materials, which contains no gold, was by far the best hedge, showing a positive return in six of the seven quarters that bonds were off.

NATURAL RESOURCES FUNDS

QUARTER	VAN. BOND	FID. IND.	VAN. GOLD	NEW ERA
2Q '87	−2.21	3.75	−3.45	2.14
3Q '87	−3.11	14.66	21.48	13.26
1Q '90	−1.08	−3.22	−7.59	−1.52
1Q '92	−1.27	7.54	−4.02	−5.60
4Q '93	−0.20	11.74	31.20	5.64
1Q '94	−2.71	2.88	−6.99	−1.38
2Q '94	−1.02	3.71	−0.94	1.95

DON'T hold on to a fund that has changed direction.

If you've taken care in putting together your portfolio of mutual funds, you've selected funds that complement one another. Now you want all the portfolio managers you've chosen to do their job. Unfortunately, many of them tend to change direction when returns fall off in their own arena. For example, in the 1990s, many U.S. growth funds began moving their assets overseas to boost returns. By 1995, these five funds had 20 percent or more of their assets overseas: Janus Fund, Strong Opportunity, Twentieth Century Growth Investor, Fidelity Retirement Growth, and Fidelity Contrafund.

Investment advisers dump funds that stray from their objectives. You should, too, if you've taken the trouble to select one fund to do one job, like invest in domestic growth stocks, and another to do something different, like invest overseas. "There are three things we look for in a fund," says Harold Evensky, an investment adviser in Coral Gables, Fla. "Philosophy, process, and people. If they change their philosophy, their process, or their people, we're out."

When a fund company announces that it plans to take a fund in a new direction, that should be your signal to leave. You don't know that it won't work out. But the fund is no longer doing what you chose it to do. For

ILLIQUID SECURITIES *Financial instruments, such as stocks of extremely small companies or stocks in developing countries where there are few traders, that cannot be traded easily.*

example, when Ryback Management took over the portfolio of the highly rated Lindner Fund in 1993, Eric Ryback, who had been assistant manager of the fund, said that he would make some changes, namely that the fund would move from small-company stocks to medium-size companies and that it would concentrate its holdings in fewer companies. But over the next couple of years, the opposite occurred, according to Morningstar. The fund actually moved to even smaller companies and doubled the number of holdings. It also moved more heavily into foreign markets.

It shouldn't matter to you whether the changes affect the performance of a fund. A change in direction alone merits action on your part. So does a request for a change in investment operations. For example, if a fund asks for more investment leeway, including the ability to trade **ILLIQUID SECURITIES** or to borrow to make investments, that should raise a red flag.

Evensky dumped the Strong Funds in 1995 when they requested broad changes in the way they were permitted to invest. He dumped the Janus Fund when it began buying foreign securities. He dropped Lindner because of its request to use illiquid securities.

The fund industry is beginning to consolidate. Mergers and acquistions of funds can make a difference. When the Colonial Funds bought Newport Tiger, which invests in the Pacific Rim, Evensky dropped it, even though he was happy with its performance; he was concerned that the big load-fund group was going to bring too much money into the fund and make it more difficult for the manager to maintain his performance.

DO leave room in your portfolio for a special manager.

One of the hottest controversies among professional investors in the 1990s is over "style drift" or "style slippage," which means a fund's drifting from one objective, such as buying U.S. small-company stocks, to another, such as buying small-company stocks around the world.

Many investment advisers hate style drift because they feel they lose control of their portfolios. That's why Harold Evensky, a Coral Gables, Fla., adviser, is a firm advocate of indexing. A former engineer, he looks at investing quantitatively. He wants each part of his portfolio in a specific box, such as "small-cap value," "emerging markets," or "small-cap growth."

But other investors, like Don Phillips, president of Morningstar Mutual Funds, feel just as strongly that a talented manager can add value. In fact, Phillips, who was a literature major at the University of Chicago, picks his funds based almost entirely on the talent of the managers. Although he thinks indexing makes good sense, to him it lacks romance.

If even the professionals can't agree, what's an average investor to do? You *should* pay attention when a fund changes direction. In other words, if a manager like Gary Pilgrim at PBHG, who has spent his entire career picking small-company growth stocks, announced that he would become a value manager, you would have little reason to stick with him.

On the other hand, I think some special managers offer something an **INDEX FUND** cannot do. There is a place in your portfolio for them. I like the approach of Eleanor Blayney, an investment adviser in McLean, Va., who uses indexes for a portfolio's core—perhaps 10 percent of assets. But she still looks for active managers to give a portfolio kick.

Even Evensky makes some exceptions. He set up a special box just for Jean-Marie Eveillard, manager of SoGen International, admitting that he couldn't justify it intellectually. "But Eveillard is just a great manager," he says.

Whom does Phillips pick as great managers?

◆ Eveillard. "You can't get this kind of talent in an index," Phillips says.

◆ Ralph Wanger, manager of the Acorn Fund, a small-company growth fund that looks around the world for offbeat ideas. When Wanger opened the Acorn International fund in 1992, Phillips signed up for a monthly investment plan. After a spectacular 1993, the fund lost 3.8 percent in 1994 and was still trailing in 1995. How long would he stick with it? "That's what my wife keeps asking me," Phillips says. The answer: a long time.

◆ John Templeton, former manager of the Templeton Growth fund, Phillips's first mutual fund, given to him by his father for Christmas when he was a child. Although Sir John no longer manages the funds, Phillips has held—and added to—his stake, which is now managed by Mark Holowesko.

◆ Peter Lynch, who established the great record of the Fidelity Magellan fund.

◆ John Neff, who retired at the end of 1995 after more than 30 years as manager of the Vanguard/Windsor fund.

◆ Michael Price, manager of the Mutual Series, a value manager with a great record.

◆ Shelby Davis, manager of Selected American Shares and New York Venture, who uses a large-cap value approach.

DON'T sell all your stock funds when you retire.

How to reposition an investment portfolio for retirement is one of the most important decisions investors must make. You have saved throughout your working years, and now is the time you must make certain your assets will last for the rest of your lifetime.

Unfortunately, many retirees are advised that the best course of action is to sell stocks or stock mutual funds and put the money in fixed-income investments. For most people, that's a mistake.

INFLATION is one of the biggest risks all investors face. It doesn't end when you retire. But your earned income does. That makes the risk of inflation much greater for retired people on a fixed income than for workers, who can hope for a pay increase, overtime, or even a higher-paying job. At age 65, you could easily have 25 or 30 years to live—and invest—but perhaps no more time to earn a salary.

Retirees don't have much flexibility in terms of generating earned income. But they do have flexibility in allocating their unearned or investment income. Even during retirement a good portion of your investments should be in stocks for growth. The average return on stocks is about 10 percent a year; for bonds it's about 5 percent.

If you can leave a good chunk of your money in stocks, you'll have more money to live on in retirement. Money that you will not need for living expenses for five years or more is a prime candidate for the stock market. Conservative blue-chip funds are a good choice. So is the Vanguard Index 500. "Our clients who are in their 60s are still 60 percent invested in stocks," says H. Lynn Hopewell, a financial planner in Falls Church, Va.

If you need to receive income from the money you've accumulated, you must move a portion of it into income-paying securities. But they need not be **BOND FUNDS**, which have problems of their own.

177

You could choose a diversified income fund like Spectrum Income, which invests in a variety of foreign and domestic bond funds and in an equity income fund. Or you might put a portion into an equity income fund itself, which invests in stocks that pay high dividends, preferred stocks, utilities, and REITs, in an effort to pay out a steady income.

Equity income funds are one of the best-performing groups of stock funds. In addition to growth and income, most offer a steady, stable performance without much volatility. T. Rowe Price, Fidelity, Vanguard, and Invesco all offer consistent good performers in this group. Lindner Dividend is another good choice.

Sheldon Jacobs, editor of *The No-Load Fund Investor,* an investment newsletter based in Irvington-on-Hudson, N.Y., compiles suggested portfolios of no-load funds for investors at different stages of life. His retirement portfolios contain a healthy dose of stocks, though they are a bit more conservative than the portfolios for workers.

Some of the funds Jacobs has recommended for retirees are: Vanguard Index 500, Mutual Beacon, T. Rowe Price International Stock, Spectrum Income, T. Rowe Growth and Income, T. Rowe Equity-Income, Vanguard/Wellesley Income, and Vanguard/Wellington.

DO check the investment style.

Investment style is one of the most controversial subjects among professional investors. Some argue that each money manager should be a purist. For example, they say that a manager should choose to buy a single asset class, such as small-company growth stocks, which means small companies that are growing rapidly. Or he should choose large-company value, that is, large companies that are undervalued by the market.

The problem is that most managers drift to where the action is. If a manager of a small-company fund sees that the real gains are to be made overseas, for instance, he might start buying foreign companies.

There are two ways to look at what the professionals call "style drift": One school says that you must insist that your manager adhere to his style. The other says that you pick a truly great manager—and there are only a handful—and let him choose whatever he likes.

Both arguments have merit. But I think you should still check to see how the fund adheres to its investment style. One good way to do that is to look at what Morningstar Mutual Funds calls its style box, printed on each fund analysis page (see example at right). This is a simple grid with nine small squares that shows whether the fund uses a value or growth approach to stock picking, or whether its style is a blend of the two, and whether it invests in large-, medium-, or small-cap stocks.

For example, Harbor Capital Appreciation fund is a large-cap growth fund. That means you can compare its performance with a market index like the S&P 500. Few large-cap funds manage to beat the index over time. Harbor Capital Appreciation is one that has since portfolio manager Spiros Segalas took over in May 1990, beating it by 24.20 in 1991 and a little over 2 percentage points in 1992, '93, and '94, and just barely in '95.

But you might want to know how Segalas has managed it. Check the investment style history. Harbor Capital Appreciation fund has been fairly consistent since Segalas took over, slipping out of large-cap growth in only one year, 1993. That's what you want to see. What you don't want to see is a fund that moves from small-company growth to large-company value and back. Look to see what portion of the fund, if any, is invested overseas. For instance, the Morningstar analysis notes that Segalas invests more than 10 percent of the portfolio in foreign-based companies. That's information you want to know.

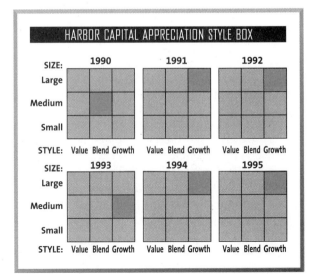

HARBOR CAPITAL APPRECIATION STYLE BOX

DO or DON'T invest with your conscience.

Why get wishy-washy at the end of the day? Socially responsible funds represent a small group that is difficult to analyze, much less to put together in a portfolio. Most investment professionals consider them part of the group of **GIMMICKY FUNDS** that rely on marketing tricks rather than investment performance to attract investors.

Here are the negatives:

◆ There are just a handful, hardly enough to make a portfolio.

◆ Performance is erratic.

◆ Many are load funds.

◆ Some use their "conscience" as a marketing tool.

◆ There is no precise definition of what a social fund is.

For example, one fund might say only that it will invest in the more responsible companies of an industry group. That still leaves a lot of room for practices that the purists might object to. Others, like the Pax World Fund, the oldest of these funds and the most austere in its restrictions, will not invest even in U.S. Treasury bonds, because some of the money is used for defense. That's why many investors suggest that you pick the best mutual funds available and then pick the charities you wish to give money to, and not mix the two.

Not everyone agrees. "Socially responsible investing eliminates a mental roadblock that some people have to investing," says Don Phillips. "Many people—some teachers and artists among them—are suspicious of the business world and see all the evils done by big business. They don't want to be party to that, so they simply don't invest at all."

That was the case with Sarah Carpenter, co-owner of Grandy Oats Granola, a breakfast-food company in Farmington, Me. When Carpenter inherited money from her father that was invested in the defense industry, she insisted on a change. "I want to feel good about what I do in this world. That means both in creating a good product and in doing what is good for me and for the environment," Carpenter says.

So, this is the single instance in which I will demonstrate ambivalence. Choosing from a broad array of funds is much better than limiting yourself to a dozen or so. That's my best advice. But if you, like Carpenter, will not invest at all if it means some of your money will go for things you cannot tolerate, consider a fund that uses "social screens," which means the managers screen stocks based on some social criteria.

Parnassus Fund has both a social conscience and a good track record. The Domini Social Equity Trust combines indexing with a social conscience. Amy Domini started with the S&P 500 and then screened out companies that she considered polluters or those that had alcohol, tobacco, gaming, nuclear power, and weapons interests. "I lost half the S&P stocks," she says. Adding 150 companies "with strong social profiles" brought her index total to 400. "When you eliminate IBM, Exxon, Du Pont, you're eliminating companies with lower financial quality than companies like Coca-Cola, Merck, and Wal-Mart," she says. The fund has under-performed the S&P 500 by just $3/10$ of one percentage point.

PART

2

BUILDING BLOCKS

I F YOU ALREADY KNOW the nuts and bolts of how mutual funds work, you can skip this section. Most investors do not. So here are some mutual fund basics, including how funds work, where they came from, and why some funds charge commissions. There are also some tips on buying, selling, monitoring, and paying taxes on funds.

One in three American households owns a mutual fund. Yet surveys show that most Americans still do not know what a mutual fund is or how it works. That's really not so surprising. Most Americans own cars, too, and yet they probably don't know how to repair them. There are some good reasons for understanding mutual funds, though. The best one is that you can save money if you choose the funds and maintain your portfolio yourself.

Here's what you need to know. A mutual fund pools the money of hundreds or thousands or even millions of different investors and uses it to buy securities, such as stocks, bonds, short-term loans in the money markets, foreign securities, or even gold or real estate. Each fund has an investment objective, which is stated in the prospectus. It might be something like "this fund seeks current income," which means the fund is designed for investors who need regular income from their investments. Or it might be "this fund seeks capital appreciation," which means it is designed for investors who want their money to grow over the long term.

In order to accomplish the objective,

the fund company hires a professional money manager to make investment decisions, trade securities, and accomplish what it is that the fund sets out to do. The way he plans to accomplish this is outlined in the prospectus.

Each investor buys a slice of this investment pool, which is called a portfolio. Investors share in the gains, losses, and expenses, according to the amount of their investment. Every day the mutual fund company calculates the value of all the assets in the portfolio. Then it deducts expenses, which include management fees, administrative costs, advertising expenses, and servicing fees, which are used to pay brokers and others who service the account. The remaining assets are divided by the number of shares outstanding to come up with the value of a single share of the mutual fund. This is called the net asset value, or NAV.

You can look up NAVs in the morning newspaper. Except in the case of closed-end funds, a fund company is obligated to buy and sell shares at the current price, or NAV, on every business day, although some funds add sales charges or redemption fees. Mutual funds pass on all their gains or losses to the shareholders. The shareholders receive two types of income from mutual fund investments: dividends and capital gains. And they pay taxes on this income as if they owned the securities outright. A mutual fund is just that simple.

Mutual funds have exploded on the American investment scene for good reason. They offer a number of advantages over investing in individual securities. Here are some of them:

Instant Diversification No matter how much or how little money you have to invest, diversification is important. You shouldn't keep all your money in the same security or even in the same market. You should have some in the large U.S. companies and some in small companies, some overseas, and perhaps some in a hedge against inflation. You should probably have a little in the money markets. (These are simply short-term loan obligations of governments, banks, and corporations. They include Treasury bills and overnight borrowings between companies.)

Most of us don't have enough money to invest in so many different securities. With a mutual fund, you can get instant diversification even if you have only $500 to invest. That's because your $500 goes into the portfolio, or pool, of money with the dollars of lots of other small investors. Even with a small investment, you might own a piece of 100 different stocks.

Marketability There is a ready buyer for your mutual fund shares—the fund itself—when you decide to sell. Many investments, including many good ones, are not readily marketable. That means you can't get your money out when you need it. For example, your house may be the best investment you've ever made. But if you need money to pay an emergency medical bill, the investment in your house won't help. Mutual funds can be sold quickly and conveniently. Each open-end fund is required to establish a daily price for shares. You can redeem your shares at that price and have the money wired to your bank by the following business day. Or you can transfer the sale proceeds from a fund into a money market fund in the same fund family and write a check on it.

Convenience You can buy mutual funds by mail and by phone, or from a broker, a bank, or an insurance agent. To make automatic, regular purchases of mutual fund shares, you can arrange to have deductions made from your paycheck or bank account. You can also elect to have your dividends and capital gains automatically reinvested in new shares of the fund. By contrast, when you buy stocks or bonds directly, earnings may sit idle in an account that earns no interest. Reinvestment, and the power of compounding, help your mutual fund investment grow much more rapidly.

Flexibility Just as you can buy and sell your funds easily, you can also move your money from one fund to another within a mutual fund family. If you choose to invest in funds through a discount brokerage, you can move from one fund family to another without penalty. You can do the same thing in your 401(k) plan. You can readjust your portfolio and adapt your investments to your own changing needs or to the changing economic environment, usually with a phone call.

Professional Management The companies that sponsor mutual funds hire professional money managers to oversee your investment. It's true that investing is more complex today and that many of us don't get information quickly enough to know when to buy and sell individual stocks. Professional money managers can do this for us. They work with teams of researchers and analysts who have direct contact with thousands of companies.

Variety There are nearly 8,000 mutual funds offered by about 650 mutual fund groups or families, and the number is constantly growing. You can pick from conservative, blue-chip stock funds; funds that aim to provide income with modest growth; or those that take big risks in the search for capital gains. If you're looking for regular income, you can pick from a huge variety of income funds that range from very conservative to those that invest in low-rated "junk" bonds. You can pick a fund that invests in a single industry, in a single country, in dozens of countries around the world, or in natural resources or real estate.

Of course, there are disadvantages to investing in mutual funds as well. Here are some:

No Guarantee Your investment in a mutual fund is not guaranteed to provide a specific return. Nor are you guaranteed that your principal won't decrease in value. There is no federal or state agency that backs mutual fund investments, for example, in the way that the Federal Deposit Insurance Corp. guarantees bank deposits. The mutual fund industry is extensively regulated by the U.S. Securities and Exchange Commission, which requires mutual funds to disclose information about their fees, past performance, and portfolio investments. But this does not guarantee that you won't lose your money in a mutual fund.

Minimum Investment Most mutual funds require an initial investment that ranges from $2,500 to $25,000, and sometimes more. That represents a real barrier for small investors. To make it easier, some funds waive their initial minimums and let you start with as little as $100 if you agree to make regular deposits of, say, $50 a month. Many funds also drop their minimums for special kinds of accounts. For example, minimums are typically lower—perhaps $250 or $500—for individual retirement accounts and custodial accounts for minors.

Sales Charges and Ongoing Fees Another

drawback of mutual funds is the complex structure of sales commissions and other fees. Up-front sales commissions can range up to 8.5 percent, which is more than brokers charge to sell individual stocks. Some funds charge stiff redemption fees when you sell your shares, or ongoing fees to cover sales expenses. In response to consumer resistance to sales charges, many fund companies have attempted to hide their commissions and other fees, making it more difficult to compare different funds.

Keeping Records and Tracking Performance Careful record keeping is important. Investors who don't keep complete records of their mutual fund purchases may find themselves paying higher taxes than they would otherwise have to pay when selling some of their shares. Also, tracking how well your mutual funds are performing requires some extra effort on your part, beyond just looking at the quoted share value in the newspaper.

No Local Branch Offices Most mutual fund companies do not maintain local branch offices. Instead, they deal with customers by mail or telephone from central or regional service centers. Even funds that sell shares through representatives in your community— stockbrokers, banks, or insurance agents—are likely to have their service offices elsewhere. If questions or problems arise concerning your account, you will have to handle them by mail or phone, not face-to-face.

WHERE THEY CAME FROM

Mutual funds have been around for a long time, at least since King William I set one up in the Netherlands in 1822. They flourished later in the century among the thrifty Scots. At about the same time, the British embraced them. Investment companies, along with the stock market, boomed in the United States in the Roaring '20s. The first mutual fund, or open-end fund, the Massachusetts Investors Trust, was started in this country in 1924. It still exists, offered by MFS Corp. in Boston. But during the bull market of the 1920s, mutual funds were eclipsed by their sister investments, the closed-end funds. Mutual funds were often used—and abused—during the 1920s stock market frenzy. For example, some portfolio managers borrowed heavily against the securities in the portfolio. When the market crashed, these funds were ruined.

Their collapse tarnished the entire industry. It also attracted the interest of the SEC, which began investigations into how mutual funds were marketed and operated. The result was the Investment Company Act of 1940, a federal law that regulates the industry today. It requires registration with and regulation by the SEC. The act is intended to provide investors with complete and accurate information about mutual funds and to protect them from abuses. The mutual fund industry today is one of the most heavily regulated in the financial services industry.

The SEC requires that the mutual fund company provide you with a prospectus that lists all the details of its investment offering. You must also be sent complete and accurate information about your investment. The SEC mandates that all mutual fund shareholders be treated equitably and that no major changes in operation be made without their approval. Investment companies must also disclose fees, commissions, and other charges.

The SEC cleaned up the mutual fund industry. And the stock market performed well during the 1950s. But it wasn't until the 1960s that the mutual fund industry really took off. This was the decade when a different type of money manager, with a "go-go" approach to stock picking, delivered returns of 50 percent and even 100 percent to mutual fund investors. Then came the 1969–70 bear market. Investors again deserted mutual funds in droves. But this time mutual fund companies began looking around for alternatives to funds that invested only in stocks. Fund companies knew that they had to offer different kinds of funds for all kinds of market environments if they wanted to prevent investors from taking their money back to the bank every time stocks took a downturn.

One of the mutual fund industry's most brilliant innovations—the money market fund— was introduced in 1971. The money market fund offered a safe, liquid alternative to banks. It paid a current market rate of interest. And it kept investors in mutual funds even if they did not want to invest in the stock market. Even though the stock market did not take off again until much later, investors started coming back to mutual funds. Many of them were small investors who had never trusted their money to anything but a bank or a savings and loan.

In the '90s, the chief source of growth in mutual funds came from the 401(k) market. As Americans began to mind their own retirement money through company-sponsored 401(k) plans, mutual fund companies rightly saw this market as the growth area going forward. At the end of 1995, there was $640 billion in 401(k) plans, according to Jeffrey Close at Access Research in Windsor, Conn. Because many studies show that 401(k) participants are less likely to move their money around than those who invest in the retail market, 401(k) plans are expected to be a source of stability for mutual funds.

WHAT'S IN A LOAD?

The financial services industry is going through a revolution in the way it offers products for sale. Banks, insurance companies, brokers, and mutual fund companies are all offering the same products. It's up to you to decide what to buy from whom. How do you buy insurance? If you're like most of us, you buy it from an agent. How do you do your banking? You probably slip your card in an ATM machine and collect the cash. What about your mutual funds? You can buy them from banks, insurance companies, brokers, discount brokers, the mutual fund companies

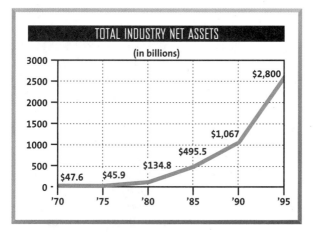

TOTAL INDUSTRY NET ASSETS
(in billions)

themselves, or through your 401(k) plan.

Fidelity Investments, the largest mutual fund company, played an interesting role in the evolution of how funds are offered to investors. Fidelity, founded in 1946, grew out of the fertile money management business that began in Boston in the 1920s. "By 1948, there were about 100 such companies in existence, with combined assets of about $1.5 billion," according to the Wiesenberger Investment Companies Services. Most of them, like Massachusetts Financial Services, Putnam Investments, and the Keystone Group, sold their products through brokers and charged investors a one-time sales commission, or "load." Scudder, Stevens & Clark was "pure no-load" from its beginning in the 1920s.

Fidelity began as a load group, offering its funds strictly through a network of broker-dealers. The story of how Fidelity came to offer its products direct differs depending on who's telling it. One source close to the company says Fidelity management became frustrated with broker-dealers' inability to sell its funds during the difficult market environment of the early 1970s and decided it could do better by selling its funds directly to the public. The pivotal event, though, was when Fidelity first offered a money market fund with check-writing privileges in 1973.

When Fidelity presented its idea to brokers, they wanted to know what the commission would be. The answer? Nothing. "The idea was to bring assets back in after the 1973 market crash," says William T. Ryan, a former Fidelity vice president, "not to pay commissions." Ryan says that when brokers rejected the no-load money fund, Fidelity decided to offer it direct.

"When the dealers said they weren't interested, we put an ad in the paper," Ryan says. "That was the inadvertent beginning of Fidelity as a direct distributor."

Although Fidelity offered its money fund direct, it was not until 1979 that it dropped the 8.5 percent load on its equity funds. Then Fidelity began to see that it could impose small loads—2 or 3 percent—even though the funds were sold direct, and the money would go straight to the fund company. It began adding loads to its most popular funds, knowing that investors would buy them anyway. In fact, it might give them even more cachet.

A story about its Magellan fund, which certainly has more cachet than any other mutual fund, with its $54 billion-plus in assets and strong performance history, illustrates this

BROKER SOLD vs. DIRECT SOLD FUNDS

	% Direct	% Sales force
1984	32.6	65.8
1985	22.9	75.6
1986	23.1	74.9
1987	27.8	69.3
1988	28.5	68.2
1989	32.6	63.5
1990	35.0	60.0
1991	34.9	59.4
1992	35.2	58.9
1993	35.8	56.8
1994	40.4	51.3
1995	36.9	53.9

Source: Investment Company Institute.
Numbers do not add up to 100 because they do not include mutual funds that are sold in variable annuities.

point. Fidelity management thought that too much money was pouring into the fund in the mid-1980s. So it decided to raise the load to 3 percent. The result? The cash inflow nearly doubled. Investors apparently reasoned that if it cost more, it had to be better. And in 1986, Fidelity introduced a new group of broker-sold funds called the Plymouth group (later renamed the Advisor series).

Fidelity is the best example of the blurring of the line between load and no-load groups, according to Catherine Voss Sanders, editor of Morningstar Mutual Funds. "It sells funds a number of ways: directly to the public without a sales charge, directly to the public with a sales charge, through registered representatives, and through its own fee-based advisory service."

Does this story have a moral? I think it is this: The idea that you "get what you pay for" does not apply to mutual funds. There is no evidence that funds with loads have anything extra to offer.

Numerous studies bolster that insight. For example, Morningstar divided its mutual fund universe into two groups in mid-1995 to study the difference between load and no-load funds. The study obviously found that load funds had a higher annual expense ratio—1.62 percent, on average, compared with 1.11 percent for no-load funds. It also found that no-load funds are a bit less aggressive, on average, in investment style. As for performance, the no-load funds outperformed in the short run when the load-fund performance was adjusted to account for loads. As the graph shows, the two groups were neck-in-neck after 10 years.

What are you to make out of this? Clearly, if you hold shares for less than 10 years, you are better off with a no-load fund. But choosing a load or no-load fund has nothing to do with performance. The fund business is extremely profitable. The more assets under management, the more money a company makes. With this in mind, fund companies structure their funds in whatever manner they feel is most likely to bring in the cash. Many funds have changed from load to no-load or vice versa. It didn't change their performance a whit.

There are two reasons to choose a load fund: you need investment advice or you have found a very special money manager who is available only in a load fund.

If you have any interest in investing, though, picking your own funds is very doable. That's partly because there is so much information available, much of it developed by Morningstar Mutual Funds, which started operations in 1984. The availability of information and heightened consumer interest has shifted the balance from broker-sold funds toward funds that are sold direct.

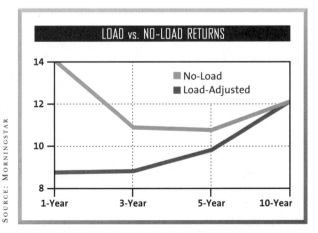

LOAD vs. NO-LOAD RETURNS

- No-Load
- Load-Adjusted

BUYING A FUND

Here are 10 questions to ask before you buy:

1. What are the expenses and fees?

2. What is the fund's ranking within its peer group for one year? Five years? Ten years?

3. Does it have a Morningstar rating? What is it? Has it changed recently?

4. What is the fund's style? Is the manager a growth picker or a value picker? You can check by looking at the "style box" in Morningstar Mutual Funds (see page 127).

5. Is the fund permitted to use derivatives? If so, how?

6. If it is a domestic fund, is it permitted to invest overseas? What percent of assets?

7. How long has the manager been with the fund?

8. How much of the assets are permitted by prospectus to be in cash? How much is currently in cash?

9. How big is the fund? Have assets increased signficantly in recent months?

10. Has anything about the fund's operation changed recently—load to no-load; expenses; 12b-1 fee; investment objective; investment parameters?

KEEPING UP

Once you've invested in a group of mutual funds, you'll need to keep tabs on them. One of the best places to get information is your daily newspaper. You'll be able to find out how the stock and bond markets moved the previous day. You'll be able to see what the short-term interest rates are doing and what money market funds are paying. And you'll be able to see how your mutual funds did, as well.

To check on your fund, look under the

"Mutual Funds" heading in the back of the business section. Major newspapers like *The New York Times* and *The Wall Street Journal* now provide different information on various days of the week. For example, on one day, the *Times* provides the fund's return for the past three months; on another, the four-week return; on yet another, the five-year average return or the Morningstar five-star rating.

First, find the name of your fund family. Let's say it's Kemper. Then find the name of the particular fund. Suppose it's Blue Chip (see example below). The "x" following the fund's name means it paid a distribution on the previous day. The "f" means it has a front-end load, or commission. The next column, which is headed NAV, shows the fund's share price at closing on the previous day—in this case, $14.01. You can see in the next column that the fund lost 1.6 percent in the previous day's trading. But it gained 29.4 percent in the

Fund Family Fund Name	NAV	Dly % Ret.	YTD % Ret.	Sales Chg.
Kemper A				
AdjRtUS xf	8.30		+ 8.1	3.50
BlueChip xf	14.01	−1.6	+29.4	5.75
Divrlnc xf	6.00	−0.5	+17.4	4.50
DremHiRet xf	20.78	−1.5	+42.0	5.75
Globlnc xf	9.52	+0.1	+19.6	4.50
Vanguard Index				
500	57.39	−1.5	+35.3	NL
Balanced	12.78	−1.2	+26.2	NL
ExtMkt	23.76	−2.1	+28.3	NL
Growth	13.93	−1.6	+37.2	NL
Inst	57.79	−1.5	+35.5	NL

year to date. That number doesn't mean much in isolation. Check to see how the U.S. stock market as a whole is doing for the year by looking up the Vanguard Index 500 (see example), which on this particular day was up 35.3 percent for the year. That means your Kemper Blue Chip fund is lagging the index. The final column shows that the sales charge is 5.75 percent for the Kemper fund. The "NL" for the Vanguard fund means it is no-load.

You already know that the net asset value is akin to the price per share of a stock. It is a figure that is recalculated daily by toting up the value of all the assets in the fund, subtracting the expenses, and then dividing the result by the number of shares in the fund.

Changes in the NAV might show you if the value of the underlying assets is increasing or decreasing. But there are other reasons for the share price to change (see page 56).

The NAV may drop when the fund declares a distribution of dividends or capital gains, or when it declares a split or dividend. This does not mean that your investment's value will drop. Instead, you will have more shares. When a fund makes a capital gains distribution, an "X" or "E" will appear after its name in the fund table. A stock dividend or split is indicated by an "S." After a distribution, you will receive a new statement. To figure the value of your investment, take the new NAV and multiply it by the number of shares you now have.

Example: Your statement shows you have 252.301 shares. The newspaper shows that your fund is trading at $15.22 per share.

252.301 x 15.22 = $3,840.02

Pay attention to the letters that pertain to sales charges and other fees, such as a 12b-1 plan. These plans make use of assets from the fund to pay for distribution and marketing charges. They might be used for advertising or to pay additional compensation to salespeople. Either way, the money comes out of the fund *before* you receive your earnings.

An "R" means that the fund has some kind of redemption fee. That means that when you sell your shares, the fund company charges you 1 percent or 2 percent. For example, let's say you invested $10,000 in a fund, left it there for 10 years, and saw it grow to $25,000. If you want to take your money out and the fund has a 1 percent redemption fee, $250 will be deducted before you receive your balance. In many newspapers, a "T" means the fund has both a 12b-1 plan and a redemption fee.

If you've chosen good funds and you're investing for the long term, you don't need to check on your funds every day. And you shouldn't be concerned if the net asset value drops a bit. Nor should you plan to sell if it gains a few cents. If you've done your home-work, you should understand that the markets move up and down from day to day and that different factors affect their performance.

But you do want to check from time to time to see that your fund is meeting its objectives. Looking at the daily price is not the way to do that. A better time to check up on your funds is each quarter, when the quarterly statistics are published in newspapers and magazines.

Look at the total return on your funds. Compare it with a couple of benchmarks. You might be interested in how the return of a large-company stock fund compares with that of the Standard & Poor's 500 Stock Index. If it is consistently below the index, you may as well buy an index fund and save money. But if you've diversified carefully, your funds are probably more specialized. You want to know how they performed compared with their peer groups.

SELLING DOS AND DON'TS

Even though you buy for the long term, there does come a time to sell. Here are 10 tips:

DO sell when it's clear that the fund is no longer doing what you bought it to do. I bought Pennsylvania Mutual Fund in 1990 because I wanted a small-company value fund and it was one of the most highly regarded. It did not do well that year, which was a bad year for small-cap stocks. I held on. The following three years, its returns were quite respectable by absolute standards. But it underperformed other small-company funds. By 1994, I had decided that it was not performing the role of a small-cap value fund, and I sold it.

DON'T set a "target price" to sell. This is a strategy that many investors use with stocks, buying when the stock hits a low and then selling when it hits a target price. Some investors do the same thing with mutual funds, believing that the fund has "peaked out." But mutual funds don't work that way. The portfolio manager is using his own buy/sell discipline. If you did your job right, you researched the fund. Then you should buy and hold.

DO sell when you're within three years of needing your money. For example, if you've saved money for your child's college education, begin to move out of stocks and into cash

three years before you will need it for tuition.
DON'T sell when the market declines. Expect
the market to move up and down.

DO sell when the portfolio manager leaves.
For example, when John Neff retired at the
end of 1995 after nearly 35 years as manager
of Vanguard/Windsor, Vanguard rightly
pointed out that his successor, Charles Free-
man, had 20 years' experience on the fund and
the transition would be smooth. Nonetheless,
as an investor, I would have sold Windsor
when Neff left.

DON'T sell on impulse. If you are becoming
disenchanted with one of your funds, do some
research. Compare its return with other funds
in its group and with a suitable index. Read the
Morningstar analysis. Try to determine if the
manager had a temporary streak of bad luck.

DO sell if the fund changes the investing rules
and you're not comfortable with the new ones.

DON'T sell a diversified stock fund because
you think it's about to end a hot streak. A
diversified stock fund should be a long-term
hold. This advice does not apply to a sector
fund. Industry sectors go in and out of favor.
Investors who use them must be able to esti-
mate when sectors will take off and decline.

DO sell if the fund moves into a different type
of security and you already have another fund
in that area.

DON'T sell when the Morningstar star rating
goes down. The rating may well have to do
with the performance of the entire class of
assets. If it is a class you want in your portfolio,
hold tight.

PART

3

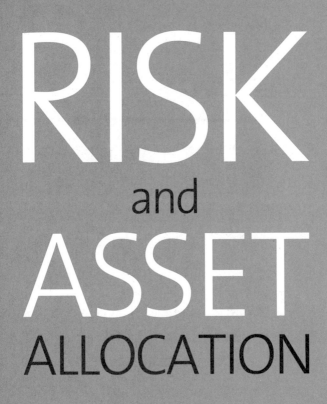

RISK
and
ASSET
ALLOCATION

OW MANY TIMES have you read that earning a good return is important, but not as important as being able to sleep at night? Investment guides typically advise you that feeling comfortable with investing is as important as earning a good return. I think that lets investors off the hook too easily. Those who don't want to learn about investing can simply claim they have a low tolerance for risk.

The truth is that no one wants to lose money. Inexperienced investors see risk in very simple terms: If I invest $10,000, will I get my $10,000 back? If there is a chance that they might lose some of it, the risk is too great. For them, that's it for determining risk tolerance. And that limits those people to a handful of investments such as Treasury bills and money market funds.

But that's far too simplistic. Every one of us would like to put our money into something that is guaranteed and still grows at 15 to 20 percent a year. That's simply not possible. Instead, you must weigh all of the different types of risks you face with your money—including the risk that you won't have enough if you don't make some prudent investments. Then, if your risk tolerance is too low for your own financial good, you must do something to increase it. Perhaps learning more about investing might help. Or making a few small investments to get comfortable with the idea of putting money in stocks.

Investment professionals see time horizon as one of the biggest factors in determining risk tolerance. If you have 10 or 20 or 30 years to invest your money, you can afford to be a big risk taker. You can't afford not to take risk if what you mean by risk is volatility or fluctuation in value. To earn a decent return, you must learn to live with some volatility. Even if you don't invest at all, you still take on plenty of risk: the risk that you won't have enough money to do the things you want to do in the future, like buy a house, pay for college for your kids, or have a comfortable retirement.

On the other hand, just because an investment is risky doesn't mean it's good. Some risky investments are just plain foolish. And some people who sell them are looking to make a quick buck at your expense. Lots of people jump at every opportunity to take a risk without even considering whether they stand a chance to do well with the investment.

I don't think people have an innate "risk tolerance" that they're born with and destined to live with. Instead, you have something of a risk profile, which goes deeper than the willingness to take a calculated chance with your money. It includes the type of decisions you make about your job, your career, your family, and where you live. It might include deciding how many children to have—or even whether to have a child, if you are financially strapped.

Although studies show that the willingness to take physical risk—like skydiving or driving race cars—has nothing to do with the willingness to take financial risk, other types of decisions probably do. Some people make seat-of-the-pants decisions about their careers and eagerly move forward, while others hang on to their jobs with all their might, even when the handwriting is on the wall. Some embrace all kinds of new experiences and refuse to second-guess themselves. Others painstakingly comb through everything that might go wrong if they were to decide to vacation at a different spot this year.

So when you think about your risk personality, don't focus only on whether you are willing to invest in India. Think also about how you decided whom to marry, what kind of house to buy, where you would vacation, and where you would shop.

Equally important in thinking about your risk profile are your investment knowledge and sophistication, your financial resources, and your disposable income. You should consider how much time you're willing to spend reading and learning about investments and keeping up with the investments you make. Do you enjoy it? Or would you be happier with something you could simply invest in and check on quarterly?

THE RISK QUIZ

Here is a quiz designed to get you thinking about your attitude toward risk and the amount of risk you can afford to take:

1. Your age is:
a. under 30
b. over 30 and under 40
c. over 40 and under 50
d. over 50 and under 65
e. 65 or over

2. You and your family have saved for a once-in-a-lifetime vacation. Two weeks before departure, you lose your job. You:
a. cancel your vacation
b. make plans for a modest vacation at the beach instead

c. go as scheduled, reasoning that job hunting will go better after a good vacation and that your family has been counting on it

d. extend your vacation and plan a real blow-out; this might be your last opportunity to go first-class

3. You move into a new neighborhood. You:

a. go door-to-door inviting neighbors to a barbecue on Saturday night

b. watch TV and wait for the phone to ring

c. join a church or temple and the PTA

d. answer an ad in the personals

4. Your current income is:

a. under $25,000

b. between $25,000 and $50,000

c. between $50,000 and $100,000

d. over $100,000

5. You are financially responsible for:

a. only yourself

b. older parents

c. both children and parents

d. bills split with working spouse, no kids

e. bills split with working spouse, kids both of you support

6. Your job:

a. is iffy

b. is secure with good potential for income growth

c. doesn't matter because you expect a large inheritance

d. doesn't matter because you expect to go out on your own soon

7. After you make an investment, you typically feel:

a. thrilled

b. satisfied

c. confused

d. regretful

8. You take a job at a fast-growing small company.

The first year, you are offered these employment choices. You choose:

a. a five-year employment contract

b. a $25,000 bonus

c. a 10 percent pay increase on your $100,000 salary

d. stock options (the opportunity to buy company stock at a set price) with a current value of $25,000 but the chance for appreciation

9. This statement best describes you:

a. I don't see any point in saving

b. I'd like to save something, but there's never anything left over

c. I try to tuck away a little whenever I can

d. I put away 5 percent or more of my salary regardless of other circumstances

10. You invest $10,000 in a stock that drops 10 percent in value the following day. You:

a. put in another $10,000 while it's down

b. sit tight, because you did the research

c. sell and go back to certificates of deposit

d. wait for the stock to regain the $1,000 loss and then sell when you have your money back

11. How would you describe your investment knowledge? Choose one.

a. I am a knowledgeable investor, well able to explain concepts such as standard deviation, beta, and other risk measurements to friends

b. I understand how mutual funds work, am familiar with the different types of funds, and feel confident discussing the best funds in different categories

c. I understand investment basics and the major markets, such as stocks, bonds, and money markets, and could explain to a friend how they work

d. I have only a vague idea about financial terminology

e. I never get into financial discussions, because I don't know any of the concepts

12. How would your spouse or best friend describe you as a risk taker?

a. foolhardy

b. willing to take risks after research

c. cautious

d. risk averse

e. afraid of your own shadow

13. How would you describe yourself as a consumer of investment information?

a. I am a business-news junkie, spending a few hours a day digesting investment information

b. I regularly read *The Wall Street Journal* and at least one specialized business publication, such as *Barron's* or an investment newsletter

c. I spend about 20 minutes a day on the financial pages

d. I watch the business news on television but don't understand much

e. I use the business section to walk the dog and avoid business news whenever possible

14. How far away are your major financial goals?

a. less than 2 years

b. 2 to 5 years

c. 5 to 10 years

d. more than 10 years

15. When you are faced with a major financial decision, you:

a. flip a coin

b. agonize

c. call each of your friends and ask what they would do

d. go with your gut

e. research the options

16. How do you feel when you suffer a financial loss?

a. I think I am a bad person

b. I feel guilty

c. I view it as a personal failure

d. I see it as an obstacle to be overcome

e. I almost never suffer losses, because I don't take risks that would lose me money

17. Your employer has offered one year's severance pay to the first 100 employees in your division who accept the package. You would most likely:

a. take it immediately

b. take it only if you had been researching business opportunities and felt you had a good option ready to go

c. freshen up your résumé and start looking around; you can't afford to leave now, but you're not going to wait for the other shoe to drop

d. ignore it; you intend to spend the rest of your career with this company

18. When you buy a health- or property-insurance policy, you:

a. try to get the lowest possible deductible or none at all; after all, what is insurance for?

b. raise the deductible to save the premium

c. get catastrophic coverage only

d. ignore the deductible and focus on the total lifetime coverage

19. You are the winner on a television game show. You have these choices. What do you do?

a. take $10,000

b. flip a coin; if you win, you get $35,000 in cash; if you lose, you get nothing

c. take $25,000 in prizes; you do not know what they are

d. spin a wheel and take the amount that you land on; it could be any of 15 possibilities, distributed equally from $1,000 to $50,000

20. You put 10 percent of your portfolio in emerging markets because that's where you think the

growth will come from over the next decade. Two
months later, emerging markets have declined by
20 percent. You:

a. sell

b. double your holdings

~ **c.** do nothing

___**d.** wait until the end of the year to rebalance,
adding to your stake if necessary to bring it
back to 10 percent

**21. You are buying a home. Your strategy would
probably be:**

SCORING	A.	B.	C.	D.	E.
1	5	4	3	2	(1)
2	1	2	(3)	5	
3	(4)	1	2	5	
4	1	2	3	(4)	
5	(4)	2	1	5	3
6	1	4	(2)	1	
7	5	(4)	2	1	
8	1	(3)	2	4	
9	1	2	3	(4)	
10	5	(4)	2	1	
11	5	4	(3)	2	1
12	5	(4)	3	2	1
13	5	4	(3)	2	1
14	1	2	3	(4)	
15	5	1	3	4	(2)
16	1	1	1	(4)	1
17	5	(4)	3	1	
18	1	(2)	4	3	
19	1	3	5	(4)	
20	1	5	4	(4)	
21	1	2	3	(5)	

8   17   11   21   3 ; 60

a. to buy something you can comfortably afford; you don't want to be house poor

b. to stretch a little for the house you want

c. to buy the most expensive house you can qualify for; you know your income will grow, and you don't want to feel squeezed in a couple of years

d. to borrow money from friends and relatives and ask your employer to inflate your salary so you can qualify for a bigger mortgage

WHAT IT MEANS

If you scored 90 or above, you may be a bit too much of a gambler. Prudent risk taking is a necessary part of a good investment program. But be careful to avoid foolhardy risks. If, for example, you answered that you typically feel "thrilled" after making an investment, that is a danger signal.

Scores in the 75-to-89 range indicate that you have a healthy tolerance for risk—and probably the wherewithal to take selective investment risks. If you are currently very conservative in your investments, perhaps you need to learn more. Knowledge is a necessary ingredient of prudent risk taking.

Scores in the 55-to-74 range show a moderate risk tolerance. If you are in this category, you can find good, conservative equity funds that will not generate too much volatility. But increasing your risk tolerance by learning more—and saving more—should be a goal.

If you scored 54 or under, do something now to increase your risk tolerance. Your overall score indicates that you approach many of life's situations with caution. So you probably will never invest in emerging markets or small-company growth stocks. That's O.K. But you should learn enough to feel comfortable putting money in the stock market for long-term investments. Set up a regular savings program to provide a nest egg to get started.

When you have accumulated a nest egg, set up an automatic investment program where $50 or $100 a month is transferred from your bank savings account to a conservative stock fund such as T. Rowe Price Equity-Income, Neuberger & Berman Guardian, or USAA Income Stock.

THE RISK-REWARD CONTINUUM

Most investments stretch along a risk-reward continuum from those that produce a steady, predictable income to those that offer the chance—but not the promise—of growth. Even if you don't have much experience as an investor, you've probably encountered an "income" investment and a "growth" investment. A bank passbook account is a conservative, guaranteed-income investment. If you take your principal of, say, $10,000 and put it in the bank, you are guaranteed that you will get your $10,000 back. And you are guaranteed income of perhaps 5 percent—or whatever the going rate is—for as long as it is in the bank.

Now consider a real estate investment. Let's say you take the same $10,000 and use it as a down payment on a $100,000 house. There is no guarantee that you will ever see your $10,000 again. But if the house appreciates to $120,000 in two years, you will have a $20,000 gain. Your $10,000 is now worth $30,000 (minus commissions). If you put the $10,000 in the bank, you would have income of about

$1,150 in two years. If you put the $10,000 into a house, you might have earned nothing or you might have earned $20,000, or even more.

Just what are the risks involved in investing? For many people, risk is simply the chance that a catastrophe of some kind or other will befall their investment and they will lose money. Even the slightest probability of that happening persuades them to keep everything in the bank, where it is guaranteed safe by the U.S. government.

For savers, investment decisions are simple: which bank pays the best rate? But investors need to know more about the different types of risks in order to make informed judgments. Here are some of the major types of risks you can face as an investor:

Inflation Risk The risk that your money will not be worth as much in the future. Inflation is a general and continual increase in the prices of the things you need to buy. The cost of housing, clothing, medical care, and food all increase constantly. Guaranteed investments simply do not earn enough to keep pace with inflation.

Opportunity Risk The risk that you will tie up your money in a so-so investment and lose the chance to put it into something with real growth potential. Investors who buy long-term bonds or certificates of deposit face this risk. Say you put $10,000 into a 10-year certificate of deposit paying 6 percent. Next year interest rates go up to 9 percent. But you are stuck with your 6 percent CD. You've lost the opportunity to put your money somewhere where it will earn more. The risk with a long-term bond is greater still. You can get out of the CD by paying a surrender penalty. But if you buy a long-term bond and rates go up, the value of your bond goes down. So with bonds, your principal, too, is at risk.

Reinvestment Risk The risk that you will not be able to invest your earnings, dividends, or even your principal at the same earnings rate next month or next year. For example, if you invest $10,000 in a bond that matures in 10 years and pays 7 percent, you will earn 7 percent, or $700 a year for 10 years. But what will you do with that $700? If interest rates drop to 5 percent, you will not be able to reinvest it at 7 percent. When your $10,000 bond matures in 10 years, you may not be able to reinvest your principal at the same rate either.

Reinvestment risk was a big problem for retirees who bought long-term fixed investments in the early 1980s when interest rates were in the double digits. Rates fell throughout the '80s (see graph at right). When those bonds came due, the money could not be invested at the same high rate. So retirees who had come to expect a high income from their investments watched that income slip away.

Reinvestment risk is a big factor for long-term investments. Clearly, the best time to buy one is when rates peak. For example, in 1982, you could have bought a long-term bank CD with an interest rate of 14 percent.

Concentration Risk With eggs (too many in one basket) as with money (too much in one stock), concentration means more risk. Portfolios containing many investments carry less risk than those with only a few, because the diversification reduces the effects of losses or gains on any particular investment.

Mutual funds provide a ready-made way to diversify your holdings over a wide range of investments and thus reduce concentration risk. Large mutual funds may hold dozens or scores of different investments. A loss on one or two of them will do relatively little damage; conversely, a big gain on one or two is hardly noticed, either.

Consider this example of an investor holding a single stock bought for $10,000 and another who put $10,000 into a mutual fund owning that stock and 39 others in equal proportions. Say the stock drops from $40 a share to $8 after the company's major product is shown to cause cancer. The investor who bought the stock by itself now holds shares worth $2,000 and has lost 80 percent of his money. The mutual fund investor has a loss, too: only $200, or 2 percent of the amount invested.

But what if the company's product were a medical miracle and the stock, instead of falling, jumped by 80 percent? The first investor would now be sitting on an $18,000 nest egg. The second, who diversified the risk by

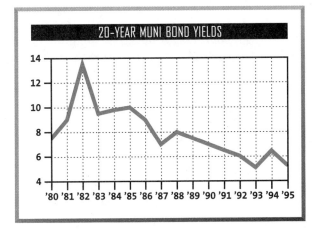

20-YEAR MUNI BOND YIELDS

choosing a mutual fund instead of direct stock ownership, would have a total of $10,200.

There are other ways of looking at concentration risk, beyond just the number of different investments you hold. Buying a dozen auto-industry stocks, for example, provides some diversification but still leaves your investments fairly concentrated in one sector of the economy. A big drop in auto sales will hurt your portfolio more than it would have if you were diversified across many economic sectors.

The same can be said of geographic concentration. If you buy only stocks of hometown companies, you may find all your investments turning sour at once if the local economy goes into a tailspin. For bond investors, maturity concentration is another important consideration. A diversified portfolio of bonds with a range of maturities, short term to long term, is less risky than one holding bonds of a single maturity. Why? Because its total value will be more stable as interest rates move up and down over the economic cycle.

Mutual funds can help you diversify your investments to reduce risk. But remember, not all mutual funds are broadly diversified. Some are concentrated in a single industry, geographic region, or bond-maturity range. That means they carry a higher degree of risk. If you're just starting out as an investor, avoid them. On the other hand, these concentrated funds—or sector funds—may carry the opportunity of a greater return and may be appropriate as one of many holdings for an investor's portfolio.

Interest Rate Risk Changes in interest rates—and in expected future interest rates— can cause the prices of some investments to rise or fall suddenly. When interest rates climb, for example, bond prices fall in lockstep. The reverse is also true: falling rates mean higher prices for bonds.

The prices of all types of investments reflect expectations about the future course of interest rates and thus to some extent are subject to interest rate risk. But the average investor is most likely to encounter interest rate risk in the bond market. If you buy a long-term bond or bond mutual fund and interest rates rise, your investment will drop in value. Should rates fall, on the other hand, you can expect to enjoy a profit as the investment gains value.

These price fluctuations can be dramatic. For example, if long-term rates double, say from 7 percent to 14 percent, the value of your bond will be cut roughly in half. You can sell it, hope to recoup something through a capital-loss tax deduction, and invest in a higher-yielding security. Or you can hold on to it, collecting 7 percent on your investment at a time when the market rate is 14 percent.

How can you reduce your exposure to interest rate risk? Pick a short-term bond fund. They're hurt less by rising rates than a long-term bond fund. What if you want to increase your exposure to interest rate risk because you think rates are going down? Buy shares in a zero-coupon bond fund. If you're right, and rates fall, you'll profit.

Credit or Default Risk Credit risk, quite simply, is the chance that a borrower won't repay an obligation. Bankers deal with it every day. You may not realize it, but as a small investor, so do you. Of the $2.8 trillion in U.S. mutual funds, more than 60 percent is invested in debt obligations, ranging in quality from U.S.

T-bills all the way down to junk bonds that pay interest not in cash but in more junk bonds.

The greater the credit risk, the greater the interest rate a borrower or issuer of securities must pay. As a result, mutual funds that invest in lower-quality securities like junk bonds offer higher yields than those that invest only in top-quality obligations like Treasury bonds. In theory, this higher yield compensates investors who are willing to take on the higher risk of loss of principal if some issuers don't repay and their bonds become worthless.

Financial experts have long debated whether the prices of various securities accurately reflect their true credit risk. Some have argued, for example, that junk bonds are a great bargain. That's because, in their view, the high junk-bond yields have overcompensated buyers for a level of credit risk that has actually turned out to be low, with fewer-than-expected losses and defaults.

Other experts criticize the prices of high-grade corporate bonds, those issued by large corporations with the top credit ratings. Their prices are out of whack, too, the critics say, not because yields are too generous but because they're too low. For only slightly less yield, these critics say, you can get a government bond with no credit risk at all.

By investing in a corporate bond fund, you get the kind of diversification that reduces your exposure to the risk of one particular company defaulting on its obligations. You can reduce risk further by picking a fund that buys only the securities of big, highly rated corporations. Or you can increase your credit risk, and your potential return, by buying shares in a junk bond fund or other type of fund that invests in low-grade debt securities.

Marketability Risk This is the chance that there will be no ready market for your investment if you want to sell it in a hurry. One of the chief advantages of mutual funds is the marketability you enjoy as a mutual fund investor. Your shares can be redeemed at any time at their net asset value per share. If you sell, you can receive cash for them in a few days, or even the next day if you have the fund company wire the proceeds from the sale directly into your bank account.

Moreover, mutual funds provide you with a way to invest indirectly in securities that would be less marketable if you bought them directly. Two examples are stocks of very small companies and mortgage securities of the Government National Mortgage Association (Ginnie Mae). The market for some small companies' stock may be inactive. Shares may trade only occasionally, and a wide spread may exist between the price being offered by sellers and what a broker will pay to take the shares off your hands. Likewise, the Ginnie Mae market features stiff charges by brokers to small investors. Buying mutual funds that specialize in small stocks or Ginnie Maes lets you participate in these investments without the marketability risk posed by owning them directly.

Because mutual funds must stand ready to repurchase shares for cash, their managers must maintain adequate cash holdings and bank credit lines to handle redemptions by any fundholders who might be selling. Funds that invest heavily in less-marketable securities, such as certain types of stock known as letter stock or restricted stock, could face problems if they are hit with a rush of redemption orders.

Currency Translation Risk Opportunities
have grown in recent years for small investors
to buy securities outside the U.S. through
international mutual funds. Many of these
investments are denominated in currencies
other than the dollar. That means the value of
your investment will change as the dollar rises
and falls relative to these other currencies. For
example, a U.S. mutual fund that invests in
Japanese securities will rise in value when the
value of the dollar falls compared with the
Japanese yen. Why? The securities denominated in the now higher-valued yen, when trans-
lated into their value in terms of the U.S. currency, buy more dollars than they did before.
The reverse is also true. A rising dollar will
hurt the value of investments denominated in
foreign currencies.

The chart below compares the risk levels of
some mutual fund investments.

SO, INVESTING IS RISKY

So is buying a house. So is working for a single
employer. And so, too, is keeping all your
money in U.S. dollars. If the dollar declines

LESS RISK/ LESS OPPORTUNITY FOR RETURN	MORE RISK/ MORE OPPORTUNITY FOR RETURN
Bond funds	Common stock funds
Stock index funds	Sector funds
Short-term bond funds	Long-term bond funds
Growth and income funds	Growth funds
T- bond funds	Zero-coupon T-bond funds
Multicountry int'l funds	One-country int'l funds
Corp. investment-grade bond funds	Corp. junk-bond funds

against other currencies, your money is worth less. Not investing is risky, too. If you are to reach your goals, you must learn to accept some risk in your investments. For the most part, that means you must invest in stocks. Getting comfortable with stock investing is worth the effort. It helps to understand how the stock market—and other investment markets—work.

In mutual funds, the risk-reward continuum starts at the low-risk, low-reward end with money market funds.

Money Market Funds The most basic mutual fund investment that provides income is a money market fund. Whatever you do with the rest of your portfolio, you will probably want to keep some of your money in a money market fund.

Money market mutual funds invest in short-term debt, or short-term "paper," issued by the U.S. Treasury, state and local governments, banks, and large corporations. So the money you invest in a money market fund is lent to government agencies or corporations.

But the loans are for very short terms, ranging from just overnight to perhaps 90 days. The SEC mandates that the average maturity of a money market portfolio cannot be more than 120 days. It also requires that money market funds invest only in the top two credit-quality grades of debt: A-1 or A-2, as listed by Standard & Poor's Corp., or P-1 or P-2, by Moody's Investor Services.

It is because the credit standards are so high for the borrowers and because the loans are for such short terms that money market funds are safe. They can be converted into cash so quickly that they are often considered to be the equivalent of cash. (When investors say that they moved out of the stock market and into a "cash position," they generally mean that they've moved their money into a money market fund.)

Because the investments made by the money market fund manager are so stable, these funds offer a fixed share price instead of one that fluctuates from day to day. In a money market fund, each share is valued at $1. So if you invest $1,000 in a money market fund, you will own 1,000 shares. Because the share price always remains at $1, you know that a money market fund will preserve your principal.

The way you earn money on these funds is through the interest they pay. The interest rate is adjusted daily to reflect changing conditions in the money market. Often these fluctuations are so tiny as to be almost unnoticeable. Still, over time, money market interest rates can change a great deal. In the early 1980s, these funds paid more than 16 percent; by the mid-'80s, they paid about 6 percent; by the late '80s, they were up to 11 percent; and in the early '90s, they were down to about 2 percent.

These are the chief advantages of money market funds:

◆ They pay competitive short-term interest rates.

◆ They are extremely safe.

◆ They are liquid. That means you can get your money out quickly and easily. You can usually write checks on a money market fund, or you can have withdrawals wired from the fund into your bank.

◆ If you use a money market account that is part of a mutual fund family, you can move money from the stock or bond market into your money fund and vice versa.

U.S. Government Securities Funds All money market funds are considered safe, although they are not guaranteed the way a bank account or a bank certificate of deposit is. The safest money market funds are those that invest only in the debt of the U.S. government. There are two kinds of government-securities money market funds. One invests only in securities issued by the U.S. Treasury. If you measure safety by the certainty that you will get your money back, this is the safest mutual fund investment you can find. The other invests in debt issued by U.S. government agencies, such as the Federal National Mortgage Association (Fannie Mae) and Ginnie Mae. Remember that we are measuring safety here by the probability that you will get your money back. The difference in safety between the government and its agencies is tiny. The difference between the government funds and those that invest in both government and corporate debt is a bit larger. A corporation could default on its debt. But the chance of that happening on the very short-term loans in the money markets is still small.

Here, then, is a lesson in how risk affects return. Because the government funds—those that buy securities of the government and its agencies—are lower risks, they will pay lower returns than money funds that include corporate debt. The difference might be between $1/10$ and $2/10$ of one percentage point, or what financial people call 10 to 20 basis points. (A basis point is $1/100$ of 1 percent.) So, for example, on a day when the Schwab Money Market fund was paying 5.36

percent, the Schwab U.S. Treasury Money Market fund was paying 5.23 percent. To figure out what this means to an investor in dollar terms, consider that if you put $1,000 in the Schwab Money Market fund (which includes government and federal agency debt, as well as bank loans and other corporate borrowings) for a year, you would earn about $53.60 (actually it would be a little more, due to the effect of compounding). If you chose instead to put your money in the Schwab U.S. Treasury Money Market fund, it would earn about $52.30.

Tax-Exempt Money Market Funds Most money market funds produce income that is taxable, just like your salary and other earnings. But some money market funds offer tax-exempt income. These funds invest in short-term municipal bonds or other municipal paper. Municipal bonds are securities issued by state and local governments and their agencies. These securities are exempt from federal tax. Bonds issued by the state where you live are also free of state taxes, and sometimes local taxes as well, if your city has them. Of course, tax-exempt money market funds pay you less income. For example, on the day that the Schwab Money Market fund paid 5.36 percent, the Schwab Tax-Exempt fund paid 3.47.

MOVING ALONG
THE CONTINUUM

Money market funds are a key investment for most people most of the time. There may be times when you want to have most of your money in the money markets. For example, if you're about to buy a house or make some other major purchase, and you want to make certain to preserve your capital, money market funds are a good choice. But when you are investing for long-term goals, like retirement or college education for your children, you need some investments that provide opportunity for growth of principal. That means you need to look beyond the money markets to the stock market and sometimes the bond market.

Bonds As you just read, money market funds invest in the money markets. Because the securities they buy are very short term, your investment is extremely liquid. Longer-term debt securities are called notes or bonds. A bond is a debt, a loan by the investor to the issuing corporation or government agency. The issuer promises to repay the principal at a specific time that might be 2 years, 10 years, or 30 years away. In addition, the issuer promises to pay interest at a specified rate. These terms are set when the bond is issued.

Bonds, too, produce income. Some investors buy bonds because they need a steady income stream. If you invest in a bond mutual fund, you can arrange to have the income either reinvested in the fund or paid to you in regular checks.

What then distinguishes a bond fund from a money market fund? Because bond funds invest in longer-term securities, they are subject to both interest rate risk and credit risk. Unlike the share price of a money market fund, the net asset value of a share in a bond fund does not hold steady. It fluctuates as the value of the bonds held in the fund changes. For example, if interest rates go up, the resale value of all outstanding fixed-rate bonds will go down, and your principal will be worth less.

Because you are taking a greater risk with your principal in a bond fund than in a money market fund, a bond fund should also pay you a higher return.

Stock Bonds are the debt of corporations or government agencies. Stock is equity, or a share of ownership, in the company. When you buy stock, you become a part owner of the company. There are no set terms or provisions to a stock investment as there are with bonds and money market funds. Stocks are likely to pay dividends. But you aren't guaranteed a specific income. And dividend income from stocks is generally much lower than interest income from bonds. When you invest in a company through a stock—or equity—mutual fund, you share in the good fortune of the companies the mutual fund manager buys, and your investment suffers if the companies fall on hard times. If a company does very well, the board of directors may decide to increase the company's stock dividend.

But the chief reason investors choose stock investments is for growth. If the economy expands and the stock market does well, a good stock mutual fund will provide growth of principal. If the stock market crashes, you will probably lose principal in a stock fund. Stock mutual funds carry a higher risk than either money market or bond funds. And they offer a higher potential reward. Over time, stocks provide a return superior to most other investments. But they are also more volatile. You should aim to put a portion of your assets into stocks to provide growth. The longer you have until you need the money, the more you should put into stocks.

There's something else you should consider

when you look at the investment markets: the concept of yield versus total return. Yield is an expression of current investment income in the form of dividends or interest. When expressed as a percent, yield refers to the annual dividend per share divided by the price of a share. Total return combines the yield, or current income, with gains or losses in principal. For example, if you own a stock with a dividend of 5 percent and the stock price goes up 5 percent, your total return is 10 percent. As an investor, you should focus on total return. With a money market fund, there is no gain or loss in principal, only current income. So the yield and the total return are the same. But with stock and bond funds, the total return can be quite different from current yield.

Although knowledge of these three markets will allow you to understand how most types of mutual funds work, some specialized funds do not invest in them or invest only in very narrow segments. These include funds that invest in gold and precious metals, in real estate, in commodity futures, or in a narrow sector of the stock market, such as high-tech companies.

These funds are more sophisticated than broadly diversified stock, bond, and money market funds. They are suitable only for investors with large portfolios who are looking for specialized investments. For more information on bond funds, see page 199; for gold funds, see pages 116 and 202; for sector funds, see page 206.

Risk Measurements Investors have developed a number of yardsticks to measure the risk of various investments, including mutual funds. None of them is perfect. They all measure risk based on past performance and cannot predict what might happen to an investment in the future. But they are useful.

Standard deviation measures the degree to which the return of a stock or a fund has varied from its average over a particular time period. Although the standard deviation measures performance in the past, it is used to project future volatility.

A high standard deviation means that the investment can be expected to have wide fluctuations in returns. For example, in 1995, Twentieth Century Ultra had a three-year average annual return of 10.14, according to Morningstar. The standard deviation for the fund during the same period was 16.75. This means that over that three-year period, roughly two thirds of the annual returns fell within a range of −6.61 to 26.89. During the same period, the Vanguard STAR fund, which is made up of a group of Vanguard funds, had an average annual return of 9.41 percent with a standard deviation of 5.57.

What can we tell from these numbers? During this particular time period, Ultra had a slightly higher annual return than STAR—73 basis points, or $^{73}/_{100}$ of 1 percent. But the volatility of Ultra was far higher. Investors who feel uncomfortable with volatility would probably be more comfortable with STAR.

Another risk measure, the beta coefficient, measures the fund's volatility relative to the S&P 500. The S&P 500 has a beta of 1. Any fund with a beta higher than 1 is more volatile than the market as a whole. For example, a fund with a beta of 1.15 is 15 percent more volatile than the S&P. If the index rises 10 percent, the fund would be expected to rise 11.5

percent (10 x 1.15). To use the same two funds as examples, Ultra has a beta of 1.26 and STAR has a beta of .65.

MEET DAVID VEENEMAN

Understanding how the markets work can help you feel comfortable with taking on more risk. Fortunately for many Americans, employers have recently become very active in investment education, partly out of self-defense.

In the early 1980s, employers began to turn responsibility for retirement savings over to employees, chiefly through 401(k) retirement savings plans. These plans allow employees to defer a portion of their income, which is usually matched to some degree by the employer. When the plans were introduced, study after study showed that employees were investing too conservatively, putting the bulk of their money in fixed-income investments with no growth potential.

Employers saw they were on the hook for educating employees when the U.S. Department of Labor introduced new rules, effective Jan. 1, 1994, that spelled out what a company must do to limit its liability if an employee did not have enough money to retire.

The rules—referred to as 404(c) regulations, for the Internal Revenue code section that lays them out—are not mandatory. But employers who comply with them will no longer be liable in the event an employee loses money because of bad investment decisions. Employers will still be responsible for picking investment managers and making certain that the options offered are good ones.

Employers who want this protection—and most do—must offer a minimum of three diversified investment options, quarterly switches between investments, and investment education so that employees understand the options.

Most employers had been leery of offering advice because they feared that if employees were told to invest in stocks and they lost money, they would blame the employer. With the 1994 rules, they saw that they could be responsible either way. Many now seek outside advisers to educate employees on their options. The goal is to help employees move out of overly conservative investments and to feel comfortable putting some of their money in the stock market.

Some employers have hired David Veeneman, a lawyer and financial planner who set up his own investment-education company and was then recruited by Hewitt Associates, an employee-benefits firm, to work with their clients' employees on investment education.

A testament to the success of Veeneman's method is the fact that, after hearing his presentation, Christine Seltz, a Hewitt principal who has been with the firm for more than 20 years, finally moved her money out of guaranteed investment contracts (GICs), an insurance company product with a guaranteed rate of return. "He's the first person who's been able to help me figure out how to allocate assets and pick equities," Seltz says.

Veeneman's focus-group work turned up several different attitudes about investing. "It's not unusual to find that two thirds of the employees are in GICs," he says. But they're not all there for the same reason. Some view investing as gambling. "The average person thinks that if they move money into equities, they could lose 100 percent," he says. Others believe that investing requires sophisticated market timing. "What they liked about the GIC was that they could pick something and stick with it."

Veeneman sees his task as making people like Seltz smarter savers rather than making them investors. What most people are afraid of, Veeneman says, is volatility, or the sharp and unpredictable movements of the market up and down—particularly down. Veeneman thinks that if people knew the likely scenario for an investment portfolio, they would feel more comfortable as investors. So he attempts to quantify this measure of investment risk by providing historical figures for volatility, with the assumption that returns will be in a similar range going forward. Veeneman also harps on the folly of jumping in and out of the stock market. "We scare them a little bit by showing

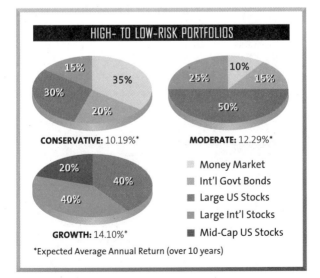

HIGH- TO LOW-RISK PORTFOLIOS

CONSERVATIVE: 10.19%*   35% / 20% / 30% / 15%

MODERATE: 12.29%*   10% / 15% / 50% / 25%

GROWTH: 14.10%*   40% / 40% / 20%

- Money Market
- Int'l Govt Bonds
- Large US Stocks
- Large Int'l Stocks
- Mid-Cap US Stocks

*Expected Average Annual Return (over 10 years)

them what a bear market feels like," Veene-man says. "We give them play money and we go through a sustained bear market." He also stresses that nobody beats the system. "We deliver a very strong message against market timing," he says.

Each portfolio is tailored to a specific 401(k) plan using that company's fund offerings. In the example on page 183, the portfolios range from conservative to aggressive.

Veeneman has had some impressive results. For example, when he did an education program at Tellabs Operations in Lisle, Ill., in June 1993, the 2,200 employees had 47 percent of their total assets in GICs and 15 percent in equities. On Sept. 30, the GIC portion had shrunk to 8 percent, and equities had been boosted to 51 percent. "We quantified the benefits of assuming risk, and that helped people feel comfortable," Veeneman says.

Good mutual fund companies provide educational materials, too. For example, Steven Norwitz, a vice president at T. Rowe Price Associates, puts together portfolios to help investors decide how to allocate assets among stocks, bonds, and cash. In the cash category, Norwitz includes assets such as Treasury bills,

STOCKS GOOSE RETURNS...

ASSET MIX			ANNUALIZED RETURN	
STOCKS	BONDS	CASH	1950-1974	1974-1994
25%	40%	35%	7.5%	10.1%
40%	40%	20%	8.6	11.2
60%	0%	10%	9.9	12.4
80%	20%	0%	11.1	13.6

SOURCE: T. ROWE PRICE

bank CDs, and money market funds.

Norwitz typically uses a 20-year period to show investors how they would have done with varying amounts of their portfolios in each of these asset classes. However, because stocks and bonds enjoyed strong bull markets during the 1980s and early '90s, he has begun using a longer historical period as well. "I didn't feel comfortable showing investors the statistics that began at the end of the 1973–74 bear market," Norwitz says. The charts on this and the previous page show four portfolios that range from 25 percent to 80 percent in stocks. The chart on the left compares their performances in the two periods; the one on the right, their historical performances.

The point I want to make here is that investors must learn to take informed risk if they are to earn good returns. Sometimes that means making mistakes in the learning process. I suspect most investors—even those we think of as the true greats, such as Warren Buffett, the billionaire from Omaha, Neb., who sometimes buys entire companies— make mistakes.

I certainly have. I bought stock at the market high in August 1987 and watched the mar-

SOURCE: T. ROWE PRICE

...AND ADD VOLATILITY

ASSET MIX STOCKS	BONDS	CASH	AVERAGE ANN.RET	BEST YEAR	WORST YEAR	# OF DOWN YRS
25%	40%	35%	7.5%	20.7%	−1.5%	3
40%	40%	20%	8.6	22.5	−6.7	8
60%	30%	10%	9.9	32.5	−13.4	8
80%	20%	0%	11.1	42.6	−20.0	10

ket crash in October of that year. I didn't stop investing in the market, but I did stop buying individual stocks. Now I buy stock mutual funds. I started with funds I considered conservative, like Lindner Dividend, and moved gradually to more aggressive funds, like PBHG Growth and Montgomery Emerging Markets. I also keep core holdings, like Mutual Shares, SoGen International, and Dodge & Cox Stock.

You and I will never be competition for Buffett, but we can be good investors. Remember that one of the chief components of risk is time. If you have the time, the volatility of the stock market will be muted and stocks will be your best investment choice.

One final note on risk: When I finished writing this part, I took my dog for a run on the streets in New York. The two of us were attacked by someone who scared off my dog and pushed me down. I broke my hip and ended up in the emergency room awaiting surgery. As I lay there, it occurred to me that the big risks we face in life are the unknown and uncontrollable ones. They make investing in the stock market look like child's play!

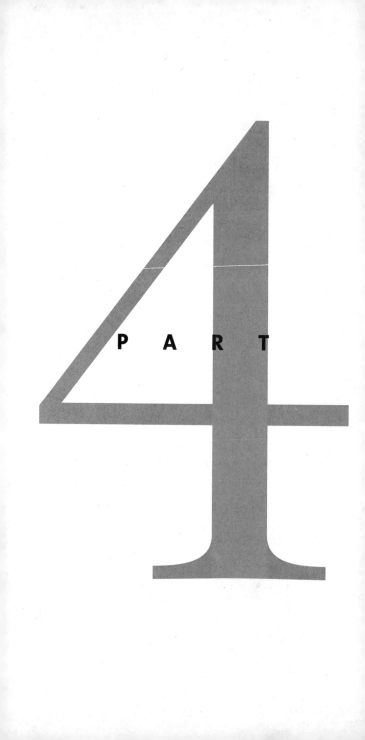

PART

4

COMMON
SENSE
STRATEGIES

SUCCESSFUL INVESTING requires discipline. The losers are those who rush into the market when it looks like everyone else is making money and then run for the exits when it sinks. Not every successful investor uses the same strategy. But every successful investor uses discipline.

It can be as simple as researching one fund and buying it to hold. Or it might be a contrarian strategy that involves buying the worst performers of the previous year. But successful investing is never haphazard. It requires a plan. Here are some strategies to consider.

BUY AND HOLD

This is where all investing should start. Buy and hold is by far the simplest—and, for most investors, the best—strategy. Jim and Priscilla Humphry, who are now in their 70s, are real people who followed this traditional investment advice and were well served by it.

Jim Humphry, who was trained as a librarian, started tucking away $100 a month in 1960. He initially picked the First Investors Fund for Income, a bond fund. Jim soon realized that bonds, which provide income, are not a good choice for a long-term investment. He wanted growth for his retirement money. To compound the problem, bonds did poorly in the '60s, with an average annual return of less than 2 percent. The fund went nowhere. "We were looking for growth, and it didn't grow," Jim says. Still, he gave it a chance, sticking with it for nearly a decade.

Then he realized that what he needed was an investment in stocks. By this time it was the early 1970s, a terrible time for the stock market. Large-company stocks returned an average of only 5.9 percent a year during the decade. But Jim had done his research and knew that, over time, stocks outperform all other investments. He picked a number of stocks and stock mutual funds and followed the same strategy: buy and hold for the long term.

By investing in a handful of good stock funds and sticking with them, he accumulated enough money to put his two daughters through college, buy them cars, pay for their weddings, and help each make a down payment on a first home.

Here is one example of how his money grew. In 1971, Jim bought 100 shares of the Smith Barney Shearson Appreciation fund for $12.50 a share, a total investment of $1,250. He has not touched that fund. At the end of 1994, he had 900 shares, worth $9,774 at $10.86 a share, thanks largely to reinvestment of dividends and capital gains. That works out to a gain of $8,524, or 682 percent, an average of 9.35 percent a year.

Jim's success was hardly due to the fact that the Smith Barney fund was the top performer over that 20-plus-year period. It was not. But like many established stock funds, it was a fine performer. By sticking with it, Jim avoided the costs associated with buying and selling.

And he avoided another mistake many investors make: selling after a bad year only to miss out on a subsequent great year. For example, in 1984, the fund gained a paltry 1.77 percent, underperforming the market as a whole. Had Jim bailed out, he would have missed the

33.96 percent gain the following year. Similarly, the fund lost 0.27 percent in 1990, but racked up a 26.94 percent gain in 1991.

The Humphrys retired comfortably and are able to spend a good deal of time traveling around the world. They did their research, picked some good funds, and stuck with them. Their success proves that it is not so much what you buy as your persistence and diligence that pay off. There is no magic to getting rich. It is simply a matter of setting money aside on a regular basis.

To follow the Humphrys' strategy:

DO pick some good growth funds with solid records.

DON'T bail out after a bad year.

DON'T use a single fund.

DO set up a portfolio of low-cost funds.

Here are some funds a buy-and-hold investor might consider: Vanguard Index 500, Dodge & Cox Stock fund, Mutual Beacon, Neuberger & Berman Guardian, T. Rowe Price Equity-Income, T. Rowe Price Spectrum Growth, Vanguard Equity-Income, Brandywine Fund, Templeton Growth, Selected American Shares.

Why are there no Fidelity funds on the list? Fidelity fields some fine funds, but the company has a tendency to shift managers around frequently, making it a poor choice, in my opinion, for buy-and-hold investors.

ROTATION

For most investors, the Humphrys' strategy works best. But for those who are a bit more adventuresome, there are ways to improve returns over the buy-and-hold strategy. One of the best ones is a contrarian strategy.

Again, you must be disciplined.

Studies show that different types of assets—such as bonds, gold, large-company stocks, and small-company stocks—move in cycles. Most investors put their money in at the very top of the cycle, just as performance for that asset has peaked, because that's when the investment gets the most attention. Remember the dazzling performance of emerging markets funds in 1993? That brought in a lot of investors just in time for those funds' whipping in 1994.

A much better strategy is to put your money into the asset that has had the worst recent performance. But you must do it systematically. You can't simply choose the worst fund of the year before. Instead, you must set up in advance the group you will work with and then plot your strategy.

For example, Jon Fossel, who is chairman of the Oppenheimer Group of funds in New York, did a study of the performance of three asset classes over the last 50 to 60 years. They were long-term bonds, small-company stocks, and utility stocks. He looked at each asset type's average annual return over the period. Then he looked at how it did in its worst 10 years. Finally, he looked at the 2 years following each of the 10 worst years. In every case, the asset performed much better following a bad year than it did in an average year.

Consider small-company stocks, which he looked at from 1934 to 1993. Small-company stocks, which are top performers over time, had an average annual return of 15.1 percent during that 60-year period. In their 10 worst years, the average decline was 22 percent. Following those bad years, small-company stocks returned an average of 21.3 percent for the next two years. So Fossel argues that an investor can improve returns by disciplined investing in the group that has recently turned in the worst performance. Here's what he found for long-term bonds in the period from 1934–93:

Avg. long-term annual return	**+5.0%**
Avg. decline in 10 worst years	**−4.3%**
Avg. annual 2-year recovery	**+7.4%**

In 1994, long-term bonds lost 12 percent, which, according to Fossel's theory, would make 1995 a good year for investing in bonds. That turned out to be the case. As interest rates dropped, the long bond gained more than 30 percent, and taxable bond funds gained an average of 15.62 percent for the year. The pattern was similar for utility stocks during the period 1945–93:

Avg. long-term annual return	**+10.4%**
Avg. decline in 10 worst years	**−7.2%**
Avg. annual 2-year recovery	**+16.8%**
1994 decline	**−15.3%**

In 1995, utility funds gained an average of 27.34, according to Lipper Analytical Services, which produces statistics on the mutual fund industry.

Fossel uses the strategy himself. When he joined Oppenheimer in 1987, he rolled over a retirement nest egg of $31,000 from his former employer and invested in the two Oppenheimer funds that had been the worst performers in 1987. He also directed all his 1988 401(k) contributions into the same two funds.

He did tinker just a bit with the list before picking his funds, though. First, he used only stock funds. Like most investment pros, Fossel, 52, believes that stocks provide the best long-term performance. The second thing he did was remove "sector" funds, those that invest in only one industry or type of security. That eliminated Oppenheimer's gold fund and Global Biotech fund from his list and left him with nine diversified stock funds.

The first year the strategy worked "spectacularly," Fossel says. He's continued it for each of the seven years he's been at Oppenheimer, moving all his retirement money into the two bottom performers.

The result? The average cumulative return of Oppenheimer's equity funds over those seven years is 118.1 percent, a tad better than the market as a whole. But Fossel's portfolio, which is now approaching a quarter of a million dollars, thanks partly to regular 401(k) contributions, has enjoyed a return of 227.7 percent over the seven years.

Had he instead selected the two top-performing funds of the previous year—a strategy that many investors use—his cumulative return would have been 73.2 percent. "It's really pretty simple," Fossel says. "You're buying low and selling high. But the end result is staggering."

Fossel's experience is hardly luck or happenstance. Although the execution is simple, the "upside-down" strategy is based on a more complex theory. Each diversified stock fund uses a different investment strategy. For example, one might invest in small-company stocks, another in international stocks, and yet another in stocks that pay high dividends. Some managers look for "growth" companies, those that are expected to grow rapidly. Others search for "value" companies, whose share prices have been beaten down based on some measure of their intrinsic value.

These different investment styles work well in different investment climates. "What happens is that there is an equilibrium price in the market," says A. Michael Lipper, president of Lipper Analytical Services. "Markets almost always get overexcited or overdepressed, and then that works itself out and prices return to the equilibrium."

That makes Fossel's strategy of choosing funds that are out of favor vastly superior to choosing the current top performers, Lipper says, although he notes that Fossel has an advantage as head of the company that runs the funds. "What Jon can feel certain of is that the funds on the bottom are reasonably well managed," he says. "He's not buying turkeys. He's buying funds that are out of favor."

Fossel acknowledges that the strategy would not work if an investor used a group of funds that included some true dogs. Over the seven years, Fossel has used every one of the funds at least once. However, he argues that the application goes far beyond his own fund group. "I thought maybe it was just us, so I tested it with another fund group with the same result," he says. "Then I tested it going back to 1985 to give me 10 years of data, and it was the same thing."

If you want to use Fossel's strategy of upside-down investing:

DO define your universe of funds before you start.

DON'T be sidetracked by "hot" performers that are not on your list.

DO set in stone a date once a year when you will "rotate."

DO consider using the two worst-performing options in your 401(k) plan for the new contributions you make the following year.

DO choose a good no-load fund group, like the Scudder Funds in Boston or T. Rowe Price in Baltimore, and set up an automatic-investment program in which you deposit money each year into the two worst-performing funds of the year before. "T. Rowe Price would be a good choice because of the variety and type of funds offered," says Don Phillips, president of Morningstar Mutual Funds.

DO assemble your own list of funds using a publication such as Morningstar Mutual Funds to select solid funds with various investment styles.

Here are some funds to consider. You'll want to do your own research.

Small-Company Growth PBHG Growth or Wasatch Aggressive Equity

Small-Company Value Crabbe Huson Equity, Mutual Discovery, T. Rowe Price Small-Cap Value, or Royce Micro-Cap

Medium-Company Growth T. Rowe Price New America or Wasatch Mid-Cap

Medium-Company Value Schafer Value or Mutual Shares

Large-Company Growth Vanguard U.S. Growth or Harbor Capital Appreciation

Large-Company Value Dodge & Cox Stock, Selected American Shares, or Vanguard Index Value

Emerging Markets Fidelity Emerging Markets, Montgomery Emerging Markets, Templeton Developing Markets

International T. Rowe Price International

Stock, Scudder International, or Warburg Pincus International Equity

DO choose one fund from each category so that you will have eight mutual funds.

DO set an annual date when you will pick the bottom two—or even three—performers.

Fossel's strategy of moving everything to the bottom two performers is a very aggressive one. If the idea appeals to you but you don't want to bet the bank, you might direct only your new contributions into the bottom performers. Or you might want to implement the strategy for only a portion of your portfolio rather than the whole thing.

It is important, though, to be certain that your funds are all solid funds in their categories and that they all have distinct—and different—styles. For example, you will notice that the funds on our list do not include any that are designed to do well in all market climates. Those are ideal for one-fund portfolios or for a core holding. What you want here are funds with different strengths and weaknesses. "You pick one fund differently than you pick a plate of 10," says Morningstar's Don Phillips. "What you want is a group of funds that are designed so that one zigs when another zags."

BETTING ON BONDS

One theme throughout this guide is that, for the most part, investors with a long time horizon should avoid bond funds, keeping the majority of their assets in different types of stock funds, perhaps a portion in income funds like Spectrum Income or Vanguard/Wellesley Income and a small portion in cash, or in short-term bond funds, like the very solid choices offered by the Vanguard Group.

But adventuresome investors might occasionally find a time when it pays to make a bet on bonds. That is when the price of bonds is out of whack relative to stocks. Investing in bonds at such a time amounts to a bet that they will appreciate relative to stock, providing investors with a capital gain. This is not a long-term buy-and-hold investment. It is a short-term bet that prices will realign themselves. That makes it an aggressive strategy for use by seasoned investors—or investment advisers.

One such time was the end of 1994, which was the first losing calendar year for bonds since 1969. "Bond prices had declined sharply during the year, but U.S. stock prices had been flat on balance," according to a study by Sanford C. Bernstein & Co., the Wall Street research and investment firm. Because the lower the price of an asset, the better its value, "an important by-product of 1994 market movements was a change in the relative value of bonds and stocks," the report said.

Bonds typically have less return potential than stocks. But the loss in bonds in 1994 created an anomaly in prices that made bonds look like a "substitute stock," Bernstein concluded. The investment firm put 8 to 10 percent of its all-stock portfolios into 10-year Treasury bonds at the beginning of 1995.

This strategy is similar to Fossel's contrarian method of investing in the worst-performing stock fund. If you were going to make a bet on bonds, January 1995 would have been one time to do it. In fact, long-term bonds were up more than 30 percent in 1995 and the average bond fund gained more than 15 percent.

If you want to bet on bonds, remember that

the longer the term, the more the bond will respond to a change in interest rates. So a 30-year bond is a better choice than a 5-year bond. Best—and most volatile—of all is a zero-coupon bond.

Zero-coupon Treasury bonds have been around since 1981. Unlike regular Treasury bonds, which make semiannual interest payments, zeros pay no coupon, or periodic interest. Instead, they are offered at a deep discount and appreciate to face value at maturity.

Zero-coupon bonds were initially pitched as a way to target a particular time when an investor would need money for, say, college tuition. The zero bonds provided the certainty that the money would be available.

But speculators use zeros as a way to bet on bonds. Remember that when interest rates fall, bond prices rise. Because it does not pay interest, a zero bond is much more volatile than a coupon bond, both on the upside and the downside. So if interest rates fall, a zero-coupon bond will enjoy much more price appreciation than a regular bond.

If you, the investor, believe that interest rates will fall and that bonds will appreciate over the next several months—and you are willing to put your money on it—you should pick the longest-term zero-coupon bond to get the most bang for your buck. The longer the maturity, the more the price will swing. If interest rates do fall as you suspect, you will be able to sell your bonds for a nice gain.

The Benham Group in San Francisco was the first to see the potential of zeros for mutual funds. In 1985, Benham set up five funds with maturities of 1990, 1995, 2000, 2005, and 2015. Today the maturities range from 2000 to

2020. Clearly, these are not diversified funds. All the bonds mature on the same date. There are only two reasons to buy them. First, because you know you will need money for a specific financial need on a specific date, and you want to know exactly how much you will have. Second, because you believe interest rates are about to decline, and you want to make a bet on them. These funds provide a low-cost way for investors to participate in the zero-coupon market.

Consider these returns for 1995:

Vanguard Total Bond Index	**+18.2**
Benham Target 1995	**+6.8**
Benham Target 2000	**+20.7**
Benham Target 2005	**+32.6**
Benham Target 2010	**+42.1**
Benham Target 2015	**+52.7**
Benham Target 2020	**+61.3**

You would have been well rewarded for your bet in 1995. The stock market, as measured by the Vanguard Index 500, was up 37.5 percent for the year, a little more than the 10-year maturity zero-coupon fund. The 25-year maturity fund was up 61.3 percent.

USING GOLD AND OBSCURE FUNDS

There is always a lot of information in the media on how to find the best all-weather funds that can be used in everyman's portfolio. There's much less information available about how to use obscure, volatile funds to beef up your portfolio.

There's good reason for that. Most investors should stop once they've put together a portfolio of core holdings. But for investors with substantial assets, high risk tolerance, and the desire for a little spice in their portfolios, special funds might have a place.

One example of an offbeat fund is the Third Avenue Value fund, managed by Martin Whitman. Whitman's strategy sounds like the stuff investment nightmares are made of. Consider this: he invests in both U.S. and foreign securities, including junk bonds. "A substantial portion of assets may be invested in securities having relatively inactive markets," according to Morningstar. That means he may have trouble getting out if prices tumble.

He also uses risky techniques. For example, he is permitted to leverage the portfolio with up to 50 percent of assets. "New purchases will likely be made in the securities of companies in depressed industries," according to the Morningstar analysis.

So what is there to like about this fund? Whitman's record. The fund, introduced in 1990, had racked up a 21.2 percent annualized return by year-end 1995. In other words, Whitman is very good at doing some very risky things. Funds like his—and others run by talented, unconventional managers—can spice up a portfolio.

Take gold funds. Gold is certainly not a good long-term investment. It pays no dividends and earns no interest; gains come only as the price goes up. Still, when you see that some gold funds rose more than 80 percent in 1987 and 90 percent in 1993—two years that were poor to middling for the stock market—and that they gained 20 percent in the first month of 1996, it does make you want to put on your thinking cap.

How can an investor use an asset class that takes such spectacular swings yet doesn't really get anywhere? Here is a disciplined strategy—developed in a conversation with Don Phillips of Morningstar—for getting in on those double-digit years and cutting your losses, too. We call it rebalancing. Here's how it works: put a specific amount of money—say $5,000—into a gold fund and rebalance at the end of each year, either selling off or adding to the fund to bring it back to $5,000. That would allow you to nearly double your money in years that were good for gold and cut your losses in the years that gold took a drubbing.

To test the strategy, I picked the Vanguard Specialized Portfolio – Gold and Precious Metals fund for a number of reasons. True to Vanguard's commitment to low expenses, this fund has an expense ratio of just 25 basis points, or $25/100$ of 1 percent. That makes the fee on our hypothetical $5,000 investment just $12.50 a year.

Equally important, manager David J. Hutchins has a predictable style, keeping the portfolio invested one third in North American mines, one third in South African mines, and one fourth in Australian mines, according to Morningstar analyst Cebra Graves. Other metal-mining stocks, bullion, and cash make up the rest of the portfolio. The advantage here is that Hutchins is not trying to time the market, offering instead a stable investment in the fortunes of gold.

To see how the investment would test out over the years, I asked Barbara Gertz at Morningstar to consider two scenarios: One investor put $5,000 into the Vanguard gold fund on

Jan. 1, 1986, and left it untouched until Dec. 31, 1995, or for 10 years. A second investor put the same amount in on Jan. 1, 1986, but adjusted at the end of each year, bringing the balance back to $5,000. So, for example, in 1986, when the fund was up 49.88 percent, this investor would pull $2,494 out of the fund at year-end. (The results do not include fees or capital gains taxes that would be paid.)

Gertz assumed that the money taken out of the fund was invested in the Vanguard Index 500. But in 1990, when the gold fund lost 19.86 percent, our second investor would have to take $993 out of the index fund to replenish the gold fund, bringing it back up to $5,000. Just to see how our gold investments compared with a stock investment, Gertz assumed that a third investor put $5,000 into the Vanguard Index 500 and left it for the entire 10-year period.

And here are our investors' results: The investor who left the $5,000 in the gold fund for a decade did the worst, with a total of

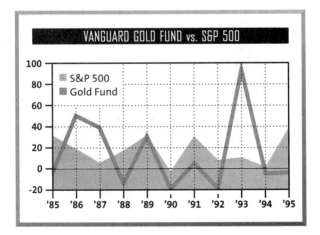

VANGUARD GOLD FUND vs. S&P 500

$13,697.10. The stock investor was second, with a total of $19,502.03. And our investor who rebalanced the $5,000 each year in the gold fund ended up with $23,211.47.

Clearly gold is not an investment for everyone. Most of us will do just as well without it. But those investors with some sense of adventure, who already have investments in the major asset classes, might want to take advantage of the volatile price swings in gold.

SECTOR INVESTING

Most investors should not own sector funds. They are volatile, unpredictable, and, worse yet, they defy the clean logic you must use to pick a mutual fund.

When you buy a sector fund, you do not look for one with a good long-term record. Sector funds are not buy-and-hold investments. Buying them means making a bet on a particular industry in the short term. Short term could mean anywhere from six months to two or three years. And sector investors must be committed to doing research on the industry they choose before they invest and then doing a lot of reading to keep abreast of changes in that industry.

There is some justification for seasoned investors to consider sectors, though. Often a particular industry leads a market advance, with stocks in that group gaining twice the market average. Sector funds allow you to make a bet on industries like biotech, financial services, or retail without taking the risk of buying a particular stock.

Sector funds have been around for years. But sector investing came of age in 1981 when Fidelity introduced the first batch of its Select funds. Since then, the number of sector funds has ballooned to a recent total of 282, according to Morningstar. Fidelity Investments still has the most, at 40; the Invesco Funds have 9. There are also some independent sector funds, like Seligman Communications.

If you look at mutual fund performance over any particular quarter—or year—chances are good that a sector fund will head the list of top performers. Chances are equally good that a sector fund will be in last place. That's why sector investing is not appropriate for most investors. It's too dicey. Buying the top-performing sector can set you up for a fall if that industry has run its course in the current cycle. "The worst mistake is to show up when the party is ending and have to pay the bill," says Albert J. Fredman, a professor at California State University in Fullerton.

How then do you pick one? Some investors simply pick the sector on the bottom, reasoning that what goes around comes around. This strategy is flawed, though. The dozens of funds available do not move in any rational pattern.

If you want to invest in sectors, you must be an active and knowledgeable investor who is willing to do some research. You might start with the sectors whose performance placed them at the bottom of the heap and find out why. For example, Fredman points out that a value investor might choose a sector fund that invests in an industry with a below-average price-earnings ratio. A growth investor might look for a hot industry on the move.

Below is a chart developed by Sam Stovall at Standard & Poor's Corp. that shows how different sectors might rotate in and out of favor during an economic cycle. This is a start. But if you want to invest in sectors, you must do more research.

KEEP IT SIMPLE

These strategies might sound far too complex to you. That's O.K. If they give you a headache, fancy investment strategies are not for you. And you don't need them. Remember that the idea of mutual funds is to simplify investing. The simplest strategy—and the one that is always successful—is buy and hold.

Remember, also, the things that you have learned about mutual funds in this guide. You

THE ECONOMIC CYCLE

One model that uses phases of the economy to predict the best sectors for investment.

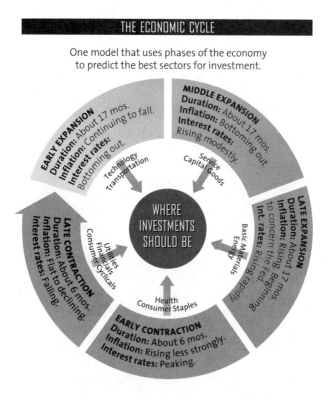

EARLY EXPANSION
Duration: About 17 mos.
Inflation: Continuing to fall.
Interest rates: Bottoming out.

Technology
Transportation

MIDDLE EXPANSION
Duration: About 17 mos.
Inflation: Bottoming out.
Interest rates: Rising modestly.

Service
Capital Goods

LATE EXPANSION
Duration: About 17 mos.
Inflation: Rising. Beginning to concern the Fed.
Int. rates: Rising rapidly.

Basic Materials
Energy

LATE CONTRACTION
Duration: About 6 mos.
Inflation: Flat to declining.
Interest rates: Falling.

Utilities
Financials
Consumer Cyclicals

WHERE INVESTMENTS SHOULD BE

Health
Consumer Staples

EARLY CONTRACTION
Duration: About 6 mos.
Inflation: Rising less strongly.
Interest rates: Peaking.

can put together a portfolio with just one fund
if you are a beginner. Even if you have a great
deal of money, a dozen funds should be
enough to get adequate diversification. Within
these boundaries, pick out a handful of good
funds representing different investment styles
that will do well in all types of market environments. And then buy them and keep them.
Good luck.

PART

5

RESOURCES

ORNINGSTAR, the Chicago rating service, is the best source of information on mutual funds for consumers (800-876-5005). The company's flagship product, which is called Morningstar Mutual Funds, is a loose-leaf binder that includes one page on each of the 1,500 funds covered. This service now costs $395 a year, which is a steep price for individual investors. It also provides more information than most of them need. In 1995 Morningstar introduced a shorter version that includes 700 no-load and low-load funds. This product, at $145 a year, is a much better choice for investors who plan to pick their own funds.

Both publications carry the same analysis. You will be able to see whether the fund you are interested in carries a load and how much it is, how big the fund is in terms of assets under management, and the net asset value. I particularly like the year-by-year performance numbers going back 10 years, which are compared with a market index such as the S&P 500 for large-company stocks or the Russell 2000 for small-company stocks. This shows me how the fund compares with a benchmark. It also shows volatility. For example, if a fund is up 55 percent one year and down 25 percent another, I might avoid it.

The performance graph indicates changes in portfolio managers with an arrow. The fund's long-term record is not so important if there's been a recent manager change.

I look at the style box, a nine-square grid that shows whether the fund buys small, medium, or large companies and whether it is growth- or value-oriented. I look at the style history, too, to see if the manager has been consistent or if he skips from one style to another. The 200-word analyses are terrific and accessible even to beginners.

I look, too, at the star rankings, which award a fund zero to five stars. The star system is based largely on the fund's recent past performance, so looking only for five-star funds is not a surefire way to pick a winner. There are good reasons to consider funds with lower rankings. For example, a good manager's style may have been out of favor and be due for a comeback.

I sometimes buy funds that are not yet rated by Morningstar, which waits until they are at least three years old. An analysis may be included on a new fund, but it will indicate that it is "not rated." Morningstar sends updates to the volume every two weeks, with commentaries by editors and surveys or studies the company has done. These are often excellent. Morningstar Mutual Funds is available in many libraries.

Really serious investors swear by Morningstar OnDisc, a CD-ROM that includes all the mutual funds available and allows investors to sort funds, set up portfolios, compare one fund to another, and so forth. The CD-ROM costs $295. If you want monthly updates, it runs $795; with quarterly updates, it costs $495. A demonstration disk is available for $5.

Look in the library, too, for the Value Line Mutual Fund Survey. Value Line is the traditional source of research on individual stocks, and the mutual fund service was introduced to compete with Morningstar's service.

OTHER PUBLICATIONS

Mutual fund investors should read the daily business pages of their local newspapers even though they need not check on the price of their mutual funds each day. Don't pay attention, though, to stories about whether the stock market is getting too high and is due for a correction. Instead you will want to keep abreast of general business news. Look, too, for items about new funds, funds that are due to open or close, and manager changes.

Most magazines today include some information on investing and personal finance, but the quality varies widely. *Money* does a good job on the basics. But ignore the "hot fund" of the month. *The Wall Street Journal* also provides good basic information on mutual fund investing, particularly in the "Getting Going" column by Jonathan Clements. I write a regular column on mutual funds for *Bloomberg Personal.* I like the straightforward, no-nonsense advice in *Kiplinger's Personal Finance* magazine too. And hard-core investors will want to subscribe to *Barron's,* the weekly journal that comes out on Saturday with news and commentary on the markets.

The American Association of Individual Investors (AAII), based in Chicago, provides excellent information for investors in its monthly journal, as well as free investment seminars for members. Some of the best investment minds in the country agree to speak at these seminars because they believe in helping to educate individual investors. For example, Jeff Vinik, manager of Fidelity Magellan fund, took a Saturday off in early 1995 to go to Chicago and speak to the AAII chapter there. To join, send $49 to AAII, 625 North Michigan Avenue, Chicago, Ill. 60611.

NEWSLETTERS

Newsletters are different from newspaper and magazine reports in that they give you advice rather than just information. An investment newsletter might tell you which funds to buy and which to sell. It might tell you to get out of the stock market and into the bond market or into cash or a money market fund. Some newsletter editors also serve as money managers, and they will manage your money for you, moving it from one fund to another. If you want to take a look at some of the newsletter options, check in *Barron's* for ads that offer trial subscriptions. My advice, though, is to learn about investing yourself and make your own decisions.

Investors who wish to subscribe to only one newsletter should choose the monthly *Morningstar Investor,* available for $79 a year. Look here for information on funds that plan to close or reopen, portfolio manager changes, and discussions of different investing styles. The centerpiece of this newsletter is the Morningstar 500, a list of 500 funds the rating agency believes have special merit.

The No-Load Fund Investor, written by Sheldon Jacobs, a longtime observer of the mutual fund industry, is also well worth the $99 subscription price for investors who want no-load funds. Jacobs includes news of new funds, recommendations, and suggested portfolios for investors depending on their goals. Write to *The No-Load Fund Investor,* P.O. Box 318, Irvington-on-Hudson, N.Y. 10533 (914-693-7420).

ON-LINE

Bloomberg on-line (www.bloomberg.com) offers some of the resources of Bloomberg Financial Markets, which are used by professionals in the financial world. The site also provides financial and world news updated continuously, and data on all types of bonds.

NETworth offers access to Morningstar data, hyperlinks to sites run by individual fund groups, and other mutual fund information. The universal resource locator (URL) is net-worth.galt.com. Similarly, the Mutual Funds Home Page (www.brill.com) is a guide to mutual fund resources on the Web.

Charles Schwab Online (www.schwab.com) provides information about Schwab's own funds, as well as OneSource (no transaction fee) funds and fund tools.

The two largest fund companies, of course, are on-line: Fidelity Investments offers information at www.fid-inv.com. Vanguard's site (www.vanguard.com) allows you to download prospectuses for funds. Vanguard also has a presence, including a bulletin board, in the Personal Finance section of America Online.

For Internet-Closed-End Fund Investor, direct your browser to www.icefi.com.

Among the features on *The No-Load Fund Investor* (www.adpad.com/noload) site is the "Wealth Builder" recommended portfolio, which is updated continually with Sheldon Jacobs's recommended no-load mutual funds.

FUND COMPANIES

Here are some resources for investors who want to buy funds on their own. They include discount brokers that offer a selection of no-

load funds, as well as toll-free numbers for
many no-load funds.

Charles Schwab OneSource	**800-435-4000**
Fidelity Funds Network	**800-544-9697**
Jack White & Co. No Fee Network	**800-323-3263**

There's a great deal of information available
from the mutual fund companies themselves.
Most publish newsletters; some of them are
very good. Many also have software programs.
Fidelity, T. Rowe Price, and Vanguard each
have a retirement-planning software program
that is available for $15.

When you receive the information, read the
prospectus and the annual report. You are
also entitled to get what the fund companies
call a Statement of Additional Information, or
Part B of the prospectus. The fund company is
required to send you a prospectus, but you
must request Part B or you will not receive it.
Part B has details on the directors and officers
and information on any person who owns 25
percent or more of the shares, as well as a
complete financial statement.

Acorn Funds	**800-922-6769**
Benham Funds	**800-331-8331**
Berger Funds	**800-333-1001**
Clipper Fund	**800-776-5033**
Cohen & Steers Realty	**800-437-9912**
Crabbe Huson Funds	**800-541-9732**
Dodge & Cox	**800-621-3979**
Dreyfus Investments	**800-645-6561**
Evergreen Asset Management	**800-235-0064**
Fidelity Investments	**800-544-8888**
Gabelli Funds	**800-422-3554**
Invesco	**800-525-8085**

Janus Capital Corp.	**800-525-8983**
Lexington Management	**800-526-0056**
Longleaf Partners	**800-445-9469**
Montgomery Funds	**800-428-1871**
Mutual Series Funds	**800-448-3863**
Neuberger & Berman Mgmt.	**800-877-9700**
Nicholas-Applegate	
Capital Management	**619-687-8100**
Parnassus Funds	**800-999-3505**
Pax World Fund	**800-767-1729**
PBHG Funds	**800-809-8008**
Robertson Stephens Funds	**800-766-FUND**
Royce Funds	**800-221-4268**
SAFECO Funds	**800-426-6730**
Scudder, Stevens & Clark	**800-225-2470**
Société Générale	
Asset Mgmt (SoGen)	**800-628-0252**
Stein Roe Mutual Funds	**800-338-2550**
Strong Funds	**800-368-3863**
T. Rowe Price	**800-638-5660**
Twentieth Century	**800-345-2021**
USAA	**800-382-8722**
Vanguard Group	**800-662-7447**
Warburg Pincus	**800-888-6878**
Wasatch Advisors Funds	**800-551-1700**

ADVISERS

Investors who need help in selecting mutual funds should look for a knowledgeable, objective adviser. For the name of a certified public accountant with a specialty in personal financial planning, call 800-TO-AICPA. For the names of certified financial planners in your area, call 800-282-PLAN.

For members of the Registry of the International Association of Financial Planners, call 800-945-IAFP (specifiy that you want only Registry members).

INDEX

ACORN FUNDS 39, 218
ALGER CAPITAL APPRECIATION 62, 89
AMERICAN ASSOCIATION OF INDIVIDUAL INVESTORS (AAII) 215-216
ANNUAL REPORT 82-83, 97
ASSET ALLOCATION 30, 32-33, 68, 96-97
ASSETS 30, 184, 194, 203
AVERAGE ANNUAL RETURN 18, 34-35

BALANCED FUND(S) 14, 18, 21
BARRON'S 82, 215-216
BASIS POINT(S) 48-49, 175
BENHAM FUNDS 218
BERGER FUNDS 218
BERNSTEIN, SANFORD C. 12, 44
BOGLE, JOHN C. 26
BOND FUNDS 12-13, 17, 21, 100-101, 125,
                            172, 177-179, 199
BONDS 10-13, 17-19, 28-31, 165-166,
                           168-170, 176-178,
                      184-185, 191, 194-195,
                           199-203, 217

CAPITAL GAINS 44-45, 57, 66-67,
                            94-95, 148
CASH 34-35, 52-53, 96-97, 144-146, 150,
                           173-174, 184-185
CATES, STALEY 44

CERTIFIED FINANCIAL PLANNER (CFP) 115
CHARLES SCHWAB & CO. 46-47, 50-51, 96, 175-176, 217-218
CLIPPER FUND 88, 111, 218
CLOSED-END FUNDS 60-61, 134, 139
CLOSED FUNDS 53
COHEN & STEERS REALTY 99, 218
COLLATERALIZED MORTGAGE OBLIGATION (CMO) 79
COMMODITY(IES) 33, 92-93
CONTRARIAN 40, 107, 190, 193, 200
CORRELATION 93, 98-99, 108-109
COST BASIS 81, 94-95
CRABBE HUSON FUNDS 218

DAVIS, SHELBY 105, 123
DERIVATIVES 78-79, 146
DIMENSIONAL FUND ADVISORS 50-51
DISCOUNT BROKER 46, 51
DIVERSIFIED FUNDS 88-89, 150-151, 179, 196
DIVIDENDS 57, 66-67, 95, 136, 148, 166, 178-179, 192, 196
DODGE & COX 14, 23, 104, 111, 186, 193, 198, 218
DOLLAR COST AVERAGING 58, 91
DOMINI SOCIAL EQUITY TRUST 129
DOW JONES AVERAGE, THE 10-11
DREYFUS INVESTMENTS 73, 218

EBRIGHT, THOMAS R. 42-43
EMERGING MARKETS 31, 39, 59, 74-77
ENCYCLOPEDIA OF CLOSED-END FUNDS, THE 61
EQUITY INCOME FUNDS 19, 125
EVEILLARD, JEAN-MARIE 33, 52, 123
EVENSKY, HAROLD 122
EVERGREEN ASSET MANAGEMENT 218

EXPENSES 16-17, 26-27, 48-51, 62, 68, 71, 101-103

FIDELITY ASSET MANAGER 21, 23, 33, 109
FIDELITY BLUE CHIP 24-25
FIDELITY CONTRAFUND 21, 109, 120
FIDELITY EQUITY-INCOME II 19, 21
FIDELITY FUNDS NETWORK 218
FIDELITY GROWTH & INCOME 21, 24, 109
FIDELITY INVESTMENTS 48, 70, 96, 112, 142, 207, 217-218
FIDELITY MAGELLAN 20-21, 52, 104, 109, 123, 215
FIDELITY PURITAN 109
FIDELITY SELECT BIOTECHNOLOGY 22-23
FINANCIAL PLANNER 114-115
FOSSEL, JON 194-197, 199-200
FOSTER HIGGINS 36-37, 107
401(K) 36, 90-91, 107, 136, 140-142, 181, 184, 195-196, 198
FPA PARAMOUNT 21, 113
FUND OF FUNDS 102-103

GABELLI, MARIO 104-105, 218
GERTZ, BARBARA 88-89, 204-205
GLOBAL FUNDS 15, 76-77
GOLD 38-39, 116-119, 202-206
GOLD FUNDS 116-117, 203
GROWTH INVESTING 110
GUARANTEED INVESTMENT CONTRACT (GIC) 91, 106-107, 182-184

HAWKINS, O. MASON 44
HEDGE(S) 31, 73, 99, 116-119
HERZFELD, THOMAS J. 61
HOLOWESKO, MARK 75, 77, 123
HOPEWELL, H. LYNN 46, 71, 125
HOTCHKIS & WILEY 19

ILLIQUID SECURITIES 120-121
INDEX FUNDS 15, 19, 21, 26-27
INFLATION 31, 98-99, 116-119, 124, 165
INITIAL PUBLIC OFFERING(S) 24, 60-61
INSTITUTIONAL FUNDS 51
INTERNATIONAL FUNDS 12, 14-15, 31,
        38, 59, 74, 76-77, 106-107, 123, 198-199
INVESCO 46, 117, 125, 207, 218
INVESTMENT CO. OF AMERICA 21
INVESTMENT STYLE 105, 126-127

JACK WHITE & CO. 46, 50-51, 96, 218
JACOBS, SHELDON 46-47, 63, 85, 125,
                                216-217
JANUS 21, 50, 59, 88, 109, 120-121, 219

KATZ, DEENA 28, 99
KAUFMANN FUND 23
KEMPER BLUE CHIP 147-148

LEHMAN BROTHERS 33, 68, 99, 118
LEXINGTON MANAGEMENT 219
LINDNER BULWARK 73
LINDNER DIVIDEND 13, 56-57, 125, 186
LIPPER, MICHAEL 197
LOAD 16-17, 48-49, 105, 112-113, 141-147
LOAD FUND 16, 112-113, 145
LONGLEAF PARTNERS 44, 53, 111, 219
LYNCH, PETER 20, 104, 123

MAGIC TRIANGLE 87
MARKET CAPITALIZATION 14, 42
MARKET TIMING 68, 73, 183-184
MERRIMAN, PAUL 68
METALS 32, 39, 117-119, 179, 204
MOBIUS, MARK 61
MONEY MARKET FUND(S) 10, 30, 36, 140,
                                146, 173-179

MONTGOMERY FUNDS 186, 219
MORNINGSTAR 12-13, 15, 17, 61, 71, 97,
           101, 113, 118, 126-127, 144-147,
             198-199, 203-204, 212-217
MUTUAL SERIES FUNDS 41, 110, 219

NATURAL RESOURCES 31, 73, 118-119, 137
NEFF, JOHN 110, 123, 151
NET ASSET VALUE (NAV) 56-57, 60-61,
             134, 147-149
NEUBERGER & BERMAN 59, 81, 164, 193,
             219
NICHOLAS-APPLEGATE CAPITAL
  MANAGEMENT 219
NO-LOAD 63-65, 112-113, 125, 144-146,
             148, 198
NO-LOAD FUND INVESTOR, THE 15, 46-47,
           53, 63, 85, 105, 125, 216-217
NORWITZ, STEVEN E. 56, 64, 78, 80,
             184-185

OPPENHEIMER 117, 194-196
OPTIONS 72

PARNASSUS FUNDS 219
PAX WORLD FUND 128, 219
PBHG 23, 53, 111, 122, 186, 198, 219
PENNSYLVANIA MUTUAL 42-43, 150
PFAMCO 50-51
PHILLIPS, DON 13, 22, 71, 91, 105, 113,
           122-123, 128, 198-199, 204
PIMCO 50-51
PORTFOLIO 14-15, 18-19, 25-27, 30-33,
      37-42, 44-48, 56-57, 59-63, 80-81, 89-91,
      96-99, 102-108, 110-111, 122-123,
        133-137, 183-184, 202-204
PORTFOLIO MANAGER 48, 62, 82-83,
           104-105, 113, 127, 150-151

PORTFOLIO TURNOVER RATE 44, 63, 83
PRICE, MICHAEL 41, 110, 123
PROSPECTUS 62-63, 133-134, 139, 146,
218
PROXY STATEMENT 70

R-SQUARED 98-99
REBALANCE 80-81, 96, 106-107, 204
REITS 13, 98-99, 125
REKENTHALER, JOHN 101, 118-119
RIGHTIME FUND 69
RIGHTS, DAVID J. 69
RISK TOLERANCE 154-156, 163
ROBERTSON STEPHENS 22, 73, 89, 219
ROYCE, CHARLES M. 42-43
ROYCE FUNDS 111, 198, 219
RUSSELL 2000 ....15, 27, 42-43, 82, 213

SAFECO FUNDS 219
SALOMON BROTHERS BOND INDEX 19
SAMS, WILLIAM 21, 113
SCHWAB ....*(see Charles Schwab & Co.)*
SCUDDER STEVENS & CLARK 49, 142, 219
SECTOR/SECTOR FUNDS 23, 38, 88-89,
106, 113, 151, 168, 179, 196, 206-208
**SECURITIES AND EXCHANGE COMMISSION
(SEC)** 16, 48-49, 63, 102, 137,
139-140, 173
SEGALAS, SPIROS 127
SHARON, ANDRE 32-33
SOGEN INTERNATIONAL 15, 19, 33, 38,
52-53, 123, 186, 219
SPECTRUM FUNDS 13, 47, 59, 102-103,
125, 193, 199
STANDARD & POOR'S 500 ....11, 14-15,
18-19, 21, 26, 37, 82, 108, 150
STEIN ROE MUTUAL FUNDS 219
STRONG FUNDS 70-71, 121, 219

T. ROWE PRICE 13, 15, 19, 46-47, 56, 59,
64, 70, 78, 80, 103, 111, 113, 119, 125,
164, 184-185, 193, 198, 218-219

TEMPLETON DEVELOPING MARKETS 61

TEMPLETON GROWTH 15, 38, 61, 75, 77,
123, 193, 198

TEMPLETON FOREIGN 15

TRAILING COMMISSION(S) 54-55

TREASURY BILLS 11, 30, 93, 135, 155, 184

12B-1 FEE 16-17, 48-49, 62, 146, 149

TWENTIETH CENTURY 23, 59, 109, 120,
180, 219

TWENTIETH CENTURY GIFTRUST 23

TWENTIETH CENTURY ULTRA 21, 59,
109, 180

USAA 13, 58, 164, 219

VALUE INVESTING 41, 110

VALUE LINE 84-85, 214

VALUE MANAGER 77, 104, 122-123

VAN WAGONER, GARRETT 15, 85, 105

VANGUARD GROUP 26, 83, 199, 219

VANGUARD INDEX 500 ...... 14, 19, 21, 26-27,
108-109, 111, 124-125, 148, 193, 202, 205

VANGUARD INDEX SMALL-CAP STOCK 27

VANGUARD/WELLESLEY 13, 125, 199

VANGUARD/WELLINGTON ... 14, 18, 109, 125

VANGUARD/WINDSOR 14, 21, 109-111,
123, 151

VEENEMAN, DAVID 181-184

VOLATILITY 10, 31, 59, 73, 75, 99, 103,
125, 156, 163, 180, 183, 185-186, 213

VINIK, JEFFREY 20, 104, 215

WALL STREET JOURNAL, THE 28, 82, 147,
160, 215

WANGER, RALPH 123

WARBURG PINCUS 15, 39, 199, 219
WASATCH ADVISORS FUNDS 219
WASHINGTON MUTUAL INVESTORS 21
WHITMAN, MARTIN 105, 203
WILSHIRE 14, 26-27, 33

YACKTMAN, DONALD 105

ZERO-COUPON BONDS 201

ABOUT THE AUTHOR

Mary Rowland is a distinguished columnist and author whose work appears in *The New York Times* as well as *Bloomberg Personal* and many other major magazines. A trusted voice in personal finance journalism, she is the author of the top-selling *Fidelity Guide to Mutual Funds*. She lives in New York City with her husband and two children.